The Sacred Light
of Healing

Also by Ron Roth

Reclaim Your Spiritual Power

Holy Spirit for Healing

I Want to See Jesus in a New Light

Holy Spirit: Boundless Energy of God

The Healing Path of Payer

Prayer and the Five Stages of Healing

Also by Roger Montgomery

Haféz: Teachings of the Philosopher of Love
(with Haleh Pourafzal)

Twenty Count: Sacred Mathematics of Awareness

The Sacred Light of Healing

✦

Teachings and Meditations on Divine Oneness

Ron Roth
With Roger Montgomery

iUniverse, Inc.
New York Lincoln Shanghai

The Sacred Light of Healing
Teachings and Meditations on Divine Oneness

iUniverse books may be ordered through booksellers or by contacting:

iUniverse
2021 Pine Lake Road, Suite 100
Lincoln, NE 68512
www.iuniverse.com
1-800-Authors (1-800-288-4677)

Because of the dynamic nature of the Internet, any Web addresses or links contained in this book may have changed since publication and may no longer be valid.

The views expressed in this work are solely those of the author and do not necessarily reflect the views of the publisher, and the publisher hereby disclaims any responsibility for them.

Cover by Becky Prelitz
www.PrelitzArt.com

ISBN: 978-0-595-44896-8 (pbk)
ISBN: 978-0-595-69059-6 (cloth)
ISBN: 978-0-595-89219-8 (ebk)

Printed in the United States of America

That all may be One in joy

Contents

Acknowledgments

The authors wish to express our deepest gratitude to His Holiness the Dalai Lama for writing the foreword for this book. We are profoundly honored by the words of this extraordinary man of peace and humility. As the light of healing and peace expands on our planet, as it must, it will owe a tremendous debt to the wisdom and compassion of this man who calls himself "just a simple monk."

For their graciousness, hospitality and warmth at the Golden City in India, Sri Amma and Sri Bhagavan will never be forgotten. Thanks also to Sri Rani Kumra for organizing our journey that would open the heart of this writing, and to dasas Ananda Giri and Pragyanand for all their guidance and help at the Oneness University.

The scientific expertise and clear explanations of Christian Opitz, both in India and now in this book, are greatly appreciated. Christian was able to take the mystery out of the blessing process while still holding the mystery of divine grace.

In addition, the authors gratefully acknowledge the extraordinary dedication of Theresa Cordova in guiding this book to publication. Theresa is a spiritual student of Ron Roth, a Celebrating Life minister, a monk in the Spirit of Peace Monastic Community and the owner of PowerofQs.com. Her perseverance was extraordinary, and we didn't make it easy for her.

The beautiful cover art is the work of Becky Prelitz, another monk and spiritual student of Ron's. Becky's painting technique is an ancient method known as *encaustic*. *Beeswax* is melted and combined with finely ground pigments and resin. This molten medium is then applied to a surface and fused. "My paintings are intended to be looking glass moments into the mysteries of the soul that lie deep within our human psyche," she explains. "The fluidity and movements strive to invoke a depth of heart rather than the mind." Her work can be seen at www.PrelitzArt.com.

An earlier version of part of Chapter 8, The Need for Discernment, appeared in the December 2005 edition of Science of Mind Magazine. Other portions of this book have appeared in The Voice of Healing, the Celebrating Life Ministries online newsletter at www.RonRoth.com, and also at www.PowerofQs.com.

Finally, we would like to thank all the spirits, saints, writers, poets and explorers of the spiritual journey whose words have contributed to our understanding of humanity's current evolution, whether or not they are identified herein.

May all beings know peace.

Foreword

By His Holiness the 14th Dalai Lama of Tibet

We are all human beings, members of one great human family sharing this planet together. We also have the same sort of experiences-when you smile at me, I feel happy, and when someone smiles at you, you feel happy. This is because we have the same basic human nature. Our future as human beings is very much interlinked and as human beings every one of us not only has the right to be happy and to live in peace, but we also have some responsibility for the happiness of others and for creating a more peaceful world.

I believe that we arrive at world peace mainly through inner peace. First the individual mind should develop peace, and this will eventually have a positive effect within his or her family and society. In this way the public can influence the leadership. While anger, hatred and aggression destroy inner peace, compassion, forgiveness, a sense of brotherhood or sisterhood, contentment, and self-discipline are its basis. Peace can develop through practice in strengthening these good inner qualities. We should then propagate this 'inner disarmament' in family life and in our schools and educational institutions.

Real peace and happiness come from within. The key to a happy life is to develop a calm and happy mind. If you have that, external circumstances will not disturb your inner peace. A traditional way to quieten the mind, to discipline and control it, is to practice prayer and meditation. Meditation is for everyone. Irrespective of whether you are a believer or an agnostic, a Buddhist or a Christian, a Hindu, a Moslem or a Jew, meditation can purify your heart and mind, leading to lasting peace and happiness.

In this book Ron Roth and Roger Montgomery explore practical steps that people can use to create and enhance inner peace within themselves and so contribute to improving not only themselves but also the world in which we live. In drawing on many methods and examples preserved in our various spiritual traditions they demonstrate how one of their greatest values is in helping us to make our lives meaningful.

According to my own limited experience, we can transform ourselves and make a difference. If we all were to spend a few minutes every day, thinking about the issues discussed here and we were to try to develop a sense of inner peace, eventually it will become part of our lives and then everything we do will contribute to peace in the wider world.

Introduction

by Roger Montgomery

Ron Roth stands as an inspirational figure to thousands who've received healing through his hands. His words in the following pages are meant to renew that inspiration for all those who love him and to offer the power of his healing touch and all-embracing universal approach to many more meeting him for the first time.

For those of you who've never met Ron, he's a former Catholic priest who felt compelled to leave that calling after twenty-five years in order to pursue a more universal spirituality. Over the next fifteen years, Celebrating Life Ministries grew up around him as an openhearted, wholistic-oriented spiritual organization, centered in Ron's public presentations. One ingredient of these presentations has been the healing energy that has poured through Ron since childhood and touched thousands, and he gained a certain amount of fame in that regard. Still, for those who've known Ron best, his never-ending search for the Divine and always present humor have marked the man most clearly.

When Ron and I began work on this manuscript in 2004, Ron typically reported that God had told him to write another book but he had no idea what it was to be about. He knew one thing, though, and that was he didn't want to write an autobiography. We began working through his recent seasons of teaching, reviewing a tall stack of lecture tapes as well as his previous writings. We completed a first draft that was far from satisfying, summarized his teachings over the years but adding little to the essence of his previous books, tapes and CDs. As always, Ron's mind was leaping forward to new spiritual vistas, and he had become fascinated with the teachings and saints of the East, my personal area of experience over many years. We began working through the basic teachings and traditions of Buddhism and Hinduism, rediscovering the wonderful correspondences with Ron's own studies of the early teachings of Jesus. He wanted these included in the manuscript.

Then came India. As reported in the early chapters ahead, Ron received an invitation to visit Indian spiritual leaders Sri Bhagavan and Sri Amma in 2005. The journey reframed and reinvigorated his life as he embraced Bhagavan and Amma's Oneness Movement, a universal plan of healing and enlightenment to help humanity prepare for its coming evolutionary destiny. This was a fresh vision of what Ron knew he'd been doing for decades. Now he knew what the book was to be about. With new insights and new purpose, we began to restructure the original draft. Then, in 2006, Ron experienced his second stroke in five years and entered a lengthy period of recovery.

Thus, this writing emerges as a compilation of particular moments of Ron Roth's reflections, lectures, contemplations, travels and meditations of recent times, set within the wide-ranging embrace of his lifetime of religious and spiritual experiences. As always, Ron embraces many aspects of spirituality, while always focusing on the opening of the Holy Spirit within. This is the telling of an extraordinary man's ongoing quest to understand the nature of what he calls the sacred light of healing. As he often has reflected, it's also been his quest to understand himself. Through this book, Ron asks all of us to join him in helping to create a better world. May all readers feel the grace of the Presence in the coming pages.

1

God in Many Forms

From the earliest days of a public ministry of forty years, the simple but powerful yearning for union with God has focused me on the pursuit of inner healing, both for myself and for others. During twenty-five years as a Roman Catholic priest and another fifteen in the healing work of Celebrating Life Ministries, I have seen my life as one joyous blessing of the Holy Spirit, an ongoing journey of exhilaration. Because many healings of physical, mental and emotional afflictions have taken place during my services and events, people insist on calling me a "healer." My response is always the same: "God heals, I do not."

That God is the true healer always has been crystal clear to me. In my services when I pray and touch people, they often react by falling to the floor and lying unable to move. This phenomenon is well known in evangelical circles as "resting in the Spirit." They lie there, often smiling, and quite a number of them report later that they have experienced both physical and emotional healings. These healings often are verified by doctors. But the process has never seemed scientific, and I could not explain what was happening. Still, I knew it was the work of God because I certainly was not personally causing these reactions and the outcomes always seemed positive. Over time, I have come to understand that this form of phenomenal healing has been practiced around the world throughout the centuries. It is the practice of bringing the sacred light to the people.

During these years of facilitating physical and emotional healings, I discovered and studied parallel teachings about the light in the sacred literature of many traditions. In recent decades, the revelations of quantum theory and other branches of science added new perspectives to understanding how humans heal, and these perspectives are aligned with the teachings of the light. But still, what precisely was happening remained locked in mysticism. In some ways, as I taught throughout the years, I often felt as uninformed about the true nature of healing as those who came to listen and to experience the energy levels that always manifested in my services. Clarity ultimately would arise, however, and it would come in an unexpected manner in an ancient land.

In the autumn of 2005, I embarked on a journey that never had I envisioned or even considered during the first sixty-eight years of my life. Though the Presence of God has been my singular driving force since childhood, I had never wanted to go to India, that sacred goal for so many spiritual travelers. Not that I did not appreciate the benefits one can reap from traveling to sacred places. A number of years ago while still a Roman Catholic priest, I traveled to Medjugorje in Bosnia-Herzegovina in the former Yugoslavia to experience the phenomena attending the reported apparitions of the Blessed Virgin Mary. More recently, I visited John of God's healing *casa* in Brazil, another site of extraordinary events emerging in the midst of divine energetics. Wonderful mystical experiences were part of my visits to both places. But the long journey to India, that ancient land of *vedas* and *yoga*, seemed a calling for a different breed of seeker.

But go to India I did, and there I encountered extraordinary people and happenings that I had yearned to encounter all my life, yet could not anticipate in my wildest dreams. My journey emerged as the most profound spiritual experience of my life. There is a place in south India known as the Golden City, created by spiritual leaders Sri Bhagavan and Sri Amma. More recently, this community has become known as the Oneness University. In visiting this exceptionally peaceful setting, a clarity and knowingness about the Presence of God filled my heart and renewed my purpose and focus as a teacher of the healing power of unconditional joy and love. As I embraced the truth of the reality I was experiencing, India awakened my soul into a timeless moment of absolute exhilaration that projected itself over a month of ecstasy and inner discovery.

The sacred light of healing is the essence of life that brings about peace, well being and the interplay of individual and world processes. In Christian terms, it's known as the Holy Spirit, and it speaks to the mystical side of what we consider our ordinary existence. This means we can be in contact with the wondrous and wise beings who have preceded us upon this earth, and we can benefit from their guidance. I daily experience and acknowledge divine assistance from this "other side" in my life and in the lives of others. Since childhood, during my years as a Roman Catholic priest and throughout these current years of Celebrating Life Ministries, I have come to know the potential that can be realized through accepting and following this guidance. The spiritual master Jesus has been with me for as long as I can remember. Padre Pio, the 20th century Italian priest and stigmatist, has been a constant presence for many years. The Indian saints Sri Shirdi Sai Baba and Sri Aurobindo have come in more recent times. In addition, other precious saints from diverse spiritual traditions have blessed Celebrating Life and me. As I will point out, these connections can be made by anyone. It's not about me. As you read on, know that whatever light touches your heart and moves you originates from this sacred source of spirit, call it whatever you will-God, Allah, the Sacred Mother, Great Spirit. For the unconditional generosity of this guidance, I am eternally grateful.

In India, I learned that literally spreading the light of healing throughout our planet is the mission of Sri Bhagavan and Sri Amma. It is a mission going forth with a singular and purposeful focus on world peace. The casting of that same sacred light upon whatever little patches of this Earth that I myself can touch, I now understand, has been my own mission and work for all these years. And it still is. This realization, which reveals itself to many at the Oneness University, has awakened a rebirth for me. My daily life and work, both past and present, are shining with a new and powerful understanding. So, sitting quite comfortably in my new and brighter perspective, I want to share with you many beautiful aspects of this mission of joy.

Paving the pathway to a common ground of understanding and healing for ourselves, our communities, our nations and the world is the purpose of this book. If that sounds ambitious, simply realize that the way to peace and healing for one person is the same as for one family, one community, one nation, one continent and one world. As you heal, you become whole, more complete than before. As this happens, you also become a conduit for God. The more divine essence that flows through all us human conduits, the more quickly and more effectively the world itself heals. The difference a single whole (or holy) person can make is amazing. Look at Gandhi, look at Mother Theresa. But even better, let's all simply look at our own beings. By developing our inner lives, by finding true peace within, we begin to create the universal state of being that in reality we all are seeking. In the words of the Dalai Lama, "We cannot achieve world peace without first achieving inner peace within ourselves."

The timeliness of these teachings of inner divinity could not be more apparent. The first step on this pathway, of course, must be taken from where we stand right now. World events of recent years, basically since 9/11, have created a culture of fear around us all. There is probably more fear being generated in our society now than at any time ever before, and nothing is more debilitating than fear. We witness the reports of both natural disasters and human-created disasters. In the aftermath of the Twin Towers attack, we have been subjected to years of intense reaction and reprisal. We see terrorism on the upswing, televised from all over the globe. No place is immune to the endless incidents of violence throughout the world. We see terrible crises enveloping developing countries. The names of the places change, but the unbelievable horror goes on and on. Nobody is safe. Children and women are no longer protected. They die with the men because the terrorists don't care. Then come the reprisals with their ensuing violence, and then the violent reactions to the reprisals. It's simply overwhelming.

An unprecedented and devastating anticipation of violence has spread over our planet. It seems impossible to watch a news program on television without having our anxieties heightened. A vicious cycle has been set in motion, and we don't know how to get out of it. If we do nothing, if we allow ourselves to submit and go numb, this culture of fear can dominate our lives.

But our fears also go beyond the dread of terrorism. I deal with many, many people who are afraid on many, many levels. They are afraid to fly, they are afraid to walk, they are afraid to go out to the store. Yes, they are afraid of bombs, they are afraid of terrorism, but they also are afraid they won't be liked. They are afraid of losing control-but they don't realize that's a good thing. If we are able simply to let go of trying to control every little thing that comes our way, amazing things transpire. We need to lose control so that God can be in control. For many of us, this is an idea that must be learned the hard way.

A dramatic inconsistency exists between our culture of fear and the wisdom teachings of the great masters. While fear runs rampant everywhere in our daily culture, still we find consistent statements throughout the world's sacred writings that say: Do not be afraid. Be of great courage. Do not fear. Do not be afraid. This cannot harm you. Over and over, this same, empowering commandment. So we must ask ourselves-what is happening? How can we live in this world without being obsessed with fear? How can we find the true meaning within these sacred teachings that command us not to be afraid? What is this gap between our sacred wisdom and our daily living, and how do we bridge the gap?

The answer is that we start building this bridge when we look within our own hearts, find God and then reach out to other people with light and love. When we do this, God acts through us and our fear vanishes. Our hearts and minds are filled with sacred purpose instead of fear, expectations and judgments. There comes an actual change in our inner being. We can feel it. This centering on God in our daily lives moves us toward personal healing as well.

This alternative approach will allow us to move toward a healing of all the frightful wounds, step away from the ongoing mass reactions, and instead get into contact with the calming, restorative power that resides deep within us. We can call this transformative power God or Brahman or Allah or Buddha or any sacred name that we prefer. But we must realize our personal key to healing rests within us, in our hearts and minds, and not in any event or action in the outside world. We must awaken our inner resources and find the special silence that calms the outer panic and noise. It is possible and even essential that we, awakening and praying together as a world culture, achieve an inner state of being that proclaims the desire for peace as our universal common ground.

As we look at our world today, we must acknowledge the devastating fear that has pervaded our existence since 9/11. However, if we can step away from that intensity for just a moment, the realization dawns that there has to be a better way of dealing with this fear than simply turning on another news report to find out what to be afraid of next. At this point, we come face to face with our spiritual foundations. We ask inward questions. How can my personal beliefs respond to this challenge? How do I get through it all? How do I summon my inner resources? What do I believe, and is that belief capable of generating a force for good in my life and in the world?

Such questions help us realize it takes more than just professing a belief in God or in any divine entity or spiritual master to find peace and make a difference in our own lives and the lives of others. Beyond simply believing, we must take the next powerful step. We also need to live as the masters have lived in order to awaken the sacred potential within ourselves. As we study ancient writings, pray, meditate, practice new ways of being and observe sacred teachings, our lives change in meaningful ways. We experience inner well being and a progressive healing on deeper and deeper levels. Our authentic self begins to emerge.

This is what the great mythologist Joseph Campbell meant when he said, "The privilege of a lifetime is to be yourself." Just realize we are not speaking of the small self, the ego, but rather of the emergence of our own true nature, that which I call the big self or true self. The realization of God comes to us in this way. As we commence to see and know this true self, the inner nature that Hindu teachers call *Atman,* God takes control of our lives in joyous, exciting, unimaginable ways. Through this personal realization of the Divine, we can meet and rise above the challenges of our human lives, including the threatening paralysis of fear.

To heal as a society or as a world, we first must heal individually. We are all wounded somehow, many by these events of recent years, and each of us is called to experience some aspect of healing. The spiritual journey that we like to talk about is really a journey toward inner wholeness on the physical, emotional and mental levels of our individual beings.

No matter the nature of our wounds, most of us realize that spiritual essence is an aspect of healing-and I emphasize "spiritual" as different from "religious." When people who don't know me find out that I have a ministry called Celebrating Life, their first question often is, "Oh, what religion are you?" And you know something? It's difficult to answer that question directly, because my work is not about any particular religion. My work is about Holy Spirit and how She operates in our lives. (To me, Holy Spirit is a person, a living being. At various times, just as when I am speaking of God, I may use "She" or "He" or "It" as a reference.) My work is prayer. As my personal relationship with God has opened and progressed over decades, it has been made clear to me that my special grace is helping other people actually experience the Divine. That's what I've been doing for many years, and that's what I want to do in this writing.

My ministry is based on the teachings of Jesus, not as formalized by any denomination of the religious establishment, but as understood and practiced by the early Christian mystics. To understand this approach, we must go back and look at those times, understand that culture, study the Aramaic language of Jesus and get to know what his words really meant. As we examine how he responded to the conditions and challenges of his own time, we begin to draw out new ways of thinking about all we deal with in our own time. From this ancient perspective, Jesus appears to us as a role model for mastering, living and teaching the sacred secrets of the ages. In studying the wisdom literature of the world, we find all the great masters walking this same path of truth, simplicity and love.

As more and more people rediscover this ancient journey of inner knowing, the outward peace we all seek begins to emerge and arise, one person at a time. It spreads first to our families, then to our friends, our communities and our countries. In time, the unity of all our personal inner beings becomes the foundation from which even world peace can spring. That which heals the individual heals the world. This vibrant, living truth of inner realization rests at the heart of all authentic spiritual traditions. We find this clearly stated in the teachings of the Buddha, the ancient Jewish texts, the Koran, the Vedas of India. It's the message of Zen meditators, of Native American spiritual teachers, of Persian mystics and of many other wisdom traditions.

My own pathway has allowed me to experience firsthand the enormous potential that every one of us carries within our individual being. We all possess the ultimate capacity to walk upon the earth as whole human beings, attuned to the will of God and living our lives as awakened people. Throughout my ministry, I have witnessed many happenings that people call miracles, healings of physical and emotional and mental and spiritual conditions. I have watched people rise from wheel chairs when touched by the presence of the Holy Spirit. Others have thrown off depression instantly after years of suffering. It has been fascinating to watch as people's healings have confounded their well-meaning doctors, families and friends who thought they could never get better. Of course, the truth is that God does the confounding, because so many people refuse to acknowledge this level of divine influence in our daily existence until they actually experience it.

As I have stated before and will state again, God heals, I do not. Holy Spirit simply acts through my life as She can act through anyone's. She has done so with many, many mystics through the ages. I'm simply a conduit for the presence of the spirit, and every one of you is a conduit as well. Every individual, no matter what your tradition, is a conduit for this Presence of the Divine because we are all sons and daughters of God. I often say that I feel that I have been "wired for God" since childhood. That is, my nervous system was tuned from an early age to the subtle ways that the Divine appears in our life, the ways in which we become aware of God acting through our authentic self. But the truth is that anyone can develop an inner state of tuning into God through study and discipline and practice.

Now, after decades of experiencing the Divine in my own life and in the lives of so many others, my work is to lay before you as clearly as possible a simple gift-a direct pathway for awakening divine light in your own life. A pathway for bringing the living, breathing grace of peace into your personal being, a peace that can meet and overcome any negativity. This has been God's own gift to me, this discovery of that which already resides in our innermost heart. This gift is the essence of the loving wisdom of Jesus and of the saints and great masters and teachers from ancient Egypt to Europe and India. This approach has been a true pathway for millennia, and it still is true today. The opening of the heart and mind in unity is what the authentic seekers of God seek. This is the direct way to peace for the individual person and ultimately for society as well.

Life is meant to be an exhilarating experience. This is my deepest belief, and I know this truth with all my heart. But in order to exist within the wonder of this exhilaration, each of us must transcend the suffering and perceived limitations of our physical existence. We do this by living in the light. There's nothing new about seeking the light. Humanity's religions and spiritual traditions have come into being over the centuries for the purpose of bringing forth this vibrancy of being for their people. No matter in what form God is seen, the aim is the same. We live on one planet, we are of one source. Even as every single person travels a different pathway into the heart of the Divine, the Divine itself retains its absolute essence. And that absolute essence is sacred light.

In the pages ahead, we shall explore this enduring teaching as it appears in the spiritual traditions of a number of ancient and modern cultures. Since the experience with Sri Bhagavan and

Sri Amma was so moving for me personally, we will start our journey at their Oneness University in India. Along the way, we will visit the ancient Egyptian monks known the Therapeutae who often are considered the first Western monastics and serve as the model for the Spirit of Peace Monastic Community that I founded several years ago. We then will look into the beautiful Medicine Buddha teachings of Tibetan Buddhism. We will examine the words of the Dalai Lama and Mahatma Gandhi, of Mother Theresa and Hildegard of Bingen. Ancient Persian mysticism, the prayer power of Solomon, the Upanishads of India, the true meaning of Pentecost and the energy of Holy Spirit revivalist movements all will contribute light to our journey. We will examine how various masters have spoken of the light, how they used it. We shall come to understand the perception of Holy Spirit as the fire of God. We will continue to feel the healing essence of the light opening our hearts. The Divine will come alive as we share together the common wisdom that has embraced humanity down through the ages and flows unendingly through the wisdom literature of the Earth.

As we gaze into all this light, we shall see God in many forms.

Meditation

Creating Peace

At the end of each chapter in this book, you will find a guided meditation. These meditations are designed to illustrate and illumine the pathway to healing and peace, both inner and outer, by realizing our authentic self and, thereby, our true relationship with God and Holy Spirit. People today like to distinguish between prayer and meditation as two different forms, thinking of prayer as talking to God and meditation as listening to God. But the ancients did not differentiate between the two. Although I sometimes speak of prayer as the pathway into the state of meditation, in this book the two terms often are used interchangeably, just as the ancients used them.

For these meditations, choose a quiet, preferably isolated spot in your home. You may want to use spiritual objects such as pictures, statues or prayer beads to facilitate your focus on the sacred. Soft inspirational music in the background can be beneficial. Find a comfortable sitting posture. If you are more flexible than I am, you can sit cross-legged like a yogi. Or you may just relax in your favorite easy chair, which is more my style. If you wish, you might record these meditations in your own voice on a tape recorder and play them back with your eyes closed.

Begin by breathing deeply a few times, then allow your normal breathing to return. Close your eyes if you are comfortable that way. If you find yourself nodding off in the middle of the meditation, you may want to keep your eyes open. Many teachings suggest that the best way to meditate is to hold the eyes in a half-open, unfocused inner gaze. Ultimately, it's whatever works best for you.

This first practice is a modification of an ancient prayer of the Essenes, those early spiritualists of Jesus' time. This meditation is designed to welcome you into your journey into the sacred light of healing and also to enhance your own capacity to project healing light out into the world. After performing the meditation, simply sit quietly and let the energy infuse you. You will know when it is time to come out of the meditation.

The basic form of this meditation, which I have taught for many years, produces a powerful flow of inner peace in terms of the mind, feelings, emotions and body. When you have finished your preliminary preparations, you are ready to begin.

You might want to start by praying simply in the words of Saint Francis, "Lord, make me an instrument of your peace." Or you may ask the Holy Spirit to infuse you with blessings and power. Welcome whatever feelings come. There is no need to judge the feelings, just know beyond question that they come from God.

Now, sitting quietly, raise your right hand and place the tip of your fingers on the area of your forehead between the eyes and just above the brow. Say aloud or silently:

Peace to my thoughts.

Feel your mind relax. Breathe in and out.
Lower your hand and touch your heart. Say:

Peace to my feelings.

Experience your feelings releasing their hold on you. Allow freedom to begin flowing through you. Breathe.
Lower your hand to your solar plexus area. Say:

Peace to my emotions.

Notice the inner dialogue quieting and perhaps even disappearing. The effect is calming, calming, more calming. Breathe. Feel the freedom.

Next, move your hand to whatever part of your body most needs physical healing. If you cannot comfortably reach that part of the body, place your hand over your heart. Say:

Peace to my body.

Feel energy flow to that body part. You may wish to hold this position for a while as the energy builds and continues to flow and heal. Breathe deeply.

Now, gently raise your hand so that the palm is about shoulder level, facing out into the world. Say:

Peace to the world.

In Buddhism, this hand gesture or *mudra* represents fearlessness. Feel the energy flowing out from your hand into the world at large.

Now envision the world as a large pond of water, and see your hand projecting a bolt of energy like lightning outward into the middle of the pond. As the energy continues through you and out into the world, envision that energy as rings rippling out through this pond of life. See the rings continuing on and on, building up momentum. Watch them become waves, splashing far out beyond your vision, carrying the energy of peace to far distant shores. Notice that the water of the pond is sparkling.

As this energy is traveling through you, feel your connection in this moment to all other beings who are praying and meditating. Feel those in local areas near you, then those progressively farther away. You are limited only by your imagination. As you realize that the web of life connects you to all beings and all places on our planet, you actually can connect to all human beings at this instant. Together, we are actively bolstering our planet's journey toward peace in a most dynamic manner.

◆   ◆   ◆

2

In the Land of Ashrams and Avatars

The call of the Divine can be startling. In my own life, the most dramatic demonstration of God's ability to awaken, inspire and stretch our human envelope occurred on the night of Valentine's Day, February 14, 2005. On that night, I lay down to sleep rather satisfied with my life as it was. And why not? I felt I was living true to myself and to God. My ministry was founded on the principle that "the only religion is the religion of love." Based in the American heartland of Illinois, I was traveling coast to coast as a speaker, teacher and author. India existed in my imagination as a wondrous foreign country of fabled spiritual teachers of centuries past and present. But my mindset was that nothing I'd ever heard could lure me into such a long, long journey. What could I possibly care about the fabled land of ashrams and avatars half a world away?

Then, all of that changed with a mysterious and unprecedented voice ringing in my inner ear. At about 11 p.m., I was dozing off peacefully into sleep when two clear, powerfully spoken words resounded deep within my being:

"Sri Bhagavan."

And the words repeated in a set of three:

"Sri Bhagavan, Sri Bhagavan, Sri Bhagavan."

The words were enunciated slowly and carefully, and repeated precisely. This continued for hours, the same words again and again, maybe fifty times: "Sri Bhagavan, Sri Bhagavan, Sri Bhagavan." Through a lifetime of listening to spiritual voices and also teaching others how to listen, nothing like this ever had happened to me. The words called up a distinct impression of India, but I did not know if I was hearing a name or a chant or what. From my brief readings in Vedic spirituality, I recalled that "Sri" was a title for spiritual teachers, and that "Bhagavan" meant something like "Lord." Beyond that, I was clueless.

But still, I knew. I knew deep in my innermost being that here was something of enormous importance. As the voice continued, I felt an absolute urgency-I just couldn't explain it.

The following morning, I couldn't wait to check out this mystery. Consulting with members of my personal staff, by noon I had learned that Sri Bhagavan was the name of an actual person, a living spiritual master in south India not far from the city of Chennai, formerly known as Madras. A few years ago, he and his wife, another spiritual master known as Sri Amma, had initiated a worldwide enlightenment project called the Oneness Movement. Their long-term purpose is to change the world for the better by influencing the mass consciousness of humanity. In the tradition of India, Bhagavan and Amma are considered to be one *Avatar* (an incarnation of a sacred being) in two bodies, rather like two sides of the same divine coin. They communicate without speaking, without even being in the same location. One always knows what the other is doing. They reside at the Oneness University, an institution they founded.

There they perform *darshan* (literally, catching sight of divinity) ceremonies. Visitors attend from around the globe. Miracles of healing and manifestation were said to be commonplace in their presence. On the local level, their focus is educating and feeding the rural poor of India.

As we investigated further, circumstances and events began to merge into a flow that would become life changing for me and others around me. An unfolding spiritual drama began to demonstrate the absolute power of the Divine to assemble far-flung elements of our world for a purpose beyond our wildest imagination. This unfolding included discovery of many similarities between my own teachings and those of Bhagavan, as they were articulated on various Internet sites. He declared that his teachings are not about religion, that he is not interested in converting anyone to anything, but rather he wants to help each person walk his or her own path with more awareness. My sentiments, precisely. I had written and proclaimed for years that my purpose was to help the Christian be a better Christian, the Jew a better Jew, the Buddhist a better Buddhist. As the similarities of our worldview revealed themselves, my feeling for Bhagavan and Amma continued to grow. Before long, the culmination of this extraordinary chain of events would manifest as a personal invitation to visit the Oneness University as the guest of Sri Bhagavan and Sri Amma.

Bhagavan's primary mission is to implement a transformation of world consciousness through the physical transfer of enlightenment from one person to another throughout the world. He has initiated this extraordinary plan on such a scale that, over the next few years, major changes for the better in world conditions would result from the efforts of a worldwide meditation force of some 64,000 people. By the year 2012, between 5,000 and 8,000 individuals would be meditating at all times in a huge Oneness Temple, now nearing completion at the Oneness University. The temple, which includes features of sacred architecture ranging from the ancient Egyptians to the ancient Mayans, will be twenty times larger than the Taj Mahal. A work force from the local population is employed in the construction. When the temple is complete and the ongoing mass meditation is in progress, that will be the time Bhagavan foresees as the initiation of a new Golden Age for humanity.

The method of spreading this enlightenment is the bestowing of a blessing called *diksha* (literally, a ritual of initiation) that, according to both Bhagavan and contemporary scientific research, transmits energy that adjusts the human brain in all recipients to function in a more enlightened and creative manner. The scientific confirmation of the changes in brain function was very important for me because I long have held the belief that true healing embraces both the spiritual and scientific aspects of our understanding. After participating in this ritual of energy transmission in their home countries, spiritual seekers are invited to the Oneness University in India. There they undergo a training process that prepares them to bestow this blessing on others. In this way, one person at a time, this blessing of peace is intended to spread through the world.

To implement his plan for enlightenment, Bhagavan named one of his most trusted disciples, an extraordinary woman known as Sri Rani, as the international director. A true universal citizen, Rani Kumra holds a masters degree in economics and has lectured at universities in Europe. She now lives in California and travels the world as part of her work for the Oneness Movement. Within three days after my hearing the voice in the night, Celebrating Life made contact with her at her home in

California. Rani greeted the connection as an answer to her own prayers for a miraculous happening to awaken America to this universal peace movement. While the movement has taken hold in numerous countries throughout the world, the United States, obviously vital to the success of any peace movement, has been slow to respond. On being contacted by Celebrating Life, Rani sent this beautiful e-mail in reply:

> I have been praying to Bhagavan for so many days to awaken Americans. My heart cries as people do not know who Bhagavan is. For four nights I have fought with Bhagavan to awaken America. Thousands of people have been going from other countries to receive the diksha of enlightenment. Today I talked to the main disciple of Bhagavan who told me, "Do not be sad, as you have not connected with the right people yet. Now you will."
>
> A few days ago, I told Bhagavan's son to tell Bhagavan and Amma to do some great miracle in the USA. I told him how helpless I feel. He only has to get the right kind of people. This is the answer to my prayers.
>
> It touched my heart when I read that Ronji gives all the credit of his healings to God. There is a divine hand in everything that is happening and will happen. I wish you could experience for yourself who Bhagavan is.
>
> Love and light,
>
> Rani
> Oneness Movement

Rani then contacted Bhagavan with the whole story, and he personally confirmed that he wanted our Celebrating Life Ministries to help pave the way for the Oneness Movement in the U.S. The first cooperative effort of this new East-West bridge took place in Sedona, Arizona, two weeks later. Sri Rani appeared at a Celebrating Life retreat and personally blessed all four hundred people in attendance with the diksha ritual. Her teaching blended beautifully into the environment of Celebrating Life, where spiritual traditions from throughout the world are transformed into sacred energetic experiences. At this point, Bhagavan issued his invitation for members of our Spirit of Peace Monastic Community to visit the Oneness University in India.

Eight of our community members arrived at the Golden City in southern India at the end of September, and we found first-hand that the Oneness Movement is as advertised. It is about peace and healing and the light. The presence of God is recognized throughout the community and in all activities of the day and night. Whether attending the darshan of Bhagavan and Amma or interacting with the *dasas* (monks), we breathed an atmosphere infused with sacred energy. The darshan, during which Bhagavan or Amma would sit quietly and periodically raise their hands to spread light among the gathering, filled each person with a vibration of wonder and peace. I had never felt so at home in my life.

The Oneness University had been founded just two years earlier at this relatively isolated site in the midst of a wilderness area in southern India. The nearby rural community, we were told, previously was mired in poverty and problems of crime, alcoholism and spousal abuse. Now it was largely transformed. With many residents employed in the construction and maintenance of the Oneness Temple and the rest of the Golden City, the quality of life had changed. Before choosing this location, Bhagavan was advised to locate his campus elsewhere because this was such a deprived and troubled area. But Bhagavan said,

"No, this is the place. If we can change this place, we can change the world." In just two years, the place had changed.

The massive meditation focus of Bhagavan's plan is based on principles Celebrating Life has been emphasizing for years, including the many studies over the past quarter-century of what is known as the "Maharishi Effect." This extensively researched principle states that small groups of meditators, amounting to as little as the square root of one percent of a given population, can create a dramatic change in the social conditions of that population's environment. The process is named for the Indian teacher Yogi Maharishi Mahesh, founder of the international Transcendental Meditation movement. It was Maharishi who originally put forth the concept and demonstrated its effectiveness. In America and in other countries as well, group meditation has been shown to reduce negative statistics such as crime rates while also positively influencing communities. At least fifty sociological studies around the world since the 1970s have confirmed the effectiveness of this gentle method for social change. As Maharishi himself stated, "Through the window of science, we see the dawn of the Age of Enlightenment." For years, I had been expressing wonder that no one created any kind of large-scale project based on these findings. Now, here is Sri Bhagavan doing this very thing, and with a universal plan for peace to boot.

To my way of thinking, the bestowal of diksha, also known as the oneness blessing, is an actual landing of the Holy Spirit in our beings. Bhagavan's word for this landing is "Presence," as in the Presence of God. When enough people get it, he asserts, the result will be the blossoming of the new Golden Age. An enlightened populace will reshape the world in terms of attitudes, politics, healing, governments, business. Really, in terms of everything.

In line with contemporary emphasis on correlations between spiritual principles and scientific research, Bhagavan emphasizes that the effect of diksha on the human brain can be measured scientifically. In other words, this mystical experience is not really so mystical. "It's all a neuro-biological process," Bhagavan explains. "The brain responds to the energy input. I am merely a technician." His explanation in brief is that the normally frantic neural activity of the parietal lobes of the brain is quieted down so that our usual mind chatter loses its obsessive quality. At the same time, the frontal lobe's activity that enhances our perception of God is increased. The result is the condition called enlightenment. Each individual hands-on touching provides the recipient with an enlightenment experience of some type or other. The immediate reaction to this touching may be quite dramatic or seemingly nothing at all. Long-term results also vary, according to each individual's life path. But the result is always positive, always a flowering of the next step of growth.

The scientific explanation of what was happening in the human brain as a result of Sri Bhagavan's energetic blessing was extremely important to me. This was true not only because I wanted to grasp precisely how Bhagavan was planning to spread enlightenment through the Oneness Movement, but also because it allowed me to view more clearly my own work over the decades and to understand what was happening with people who, in response to my own touch, would "rest in the spirit."

The source of my understanding of the scientific observations and explanation of the diksha process is research scientist Christian Opitz. A neuroscientist and psychotherapist from Germany, Christian has studied the Oneness Movement since

2004. Some of his writings were made available to me before going to India, and I found it fortunate and far beyond coincidence that he himself arrived at the Golden City a couple of days before my visit concluded. We had a wonderful talk, he demonstrated his methods of scientific measurement and he also spoke in detail about his view of the diksha experience.

"I do not believe that science can truly understand divine grace," Christian said. "There is however, a neuro-biological explanation that can help us understand how divine grace can be transmitted through a simple process such as the diksha blessing and create profound effects on the brain.

"All spiritual traditions are attempting to free human beings from suffering," he went on. "From a neurological perspective, suffering feels so real to us, simply because certain parts of the brain that are designed for struggle and not for joy are chronically overactive. Boredom, fear, emotional pain, inner conflict, feelings of inadequacy, loneliness, feeling separate from other people, life and God are all states of consciousness that coincide with intense neurological activity in certain parts of the brain and lack of activity in others."

Christian went on to explain that his research confirmed that the blessing produced the dual effects of reduced activity in the parietal lobes of the brain while increasing the activity of the frontal lobe. This is significant because the parietal lobes, located at the back of the head, are a part of the brain's mechanism that creates a basic sense of self. In most people, the intensity of activity in the parietals, which we sometimes call inner chatter, is the foundation for believing oneself to be a separate being from all other beings and also separated from God. Conversely, the frontal lobes can be our physical vehicle for transcendence. Activated in an appropriate manner, a body of research over the years shows the frontal lobes open us to what we identify as the experience of Oneness with all other beings and with God. Inner peace and freedom arise unhindered. In most people, however, the frontal lobes are either severely underactive or not activated appropriately.

"When I first heard about Sri Bhagavan's teachings and his statement that diksha deactivates the parietal lobes and activates the frontal lobes, it sounded almost too good to be true." Christian said. "So I wanted to see if these changes could be detected in a reproducible way in people receiving diksha. To make sure that the results of my research were not due to some anomaly, I joined forces with Ralf Franziskowski, M.D., an experienced doctor in the field of psychosomatic medicine. We went to Golden City, the center of the Oneness Movement and performed tests on many people in different stages of the process of awakening induced by diksha. We used two very different devices, an electromagnetic sensor that scans a person's energy field and another device measuring electrical resistance in the skin, which is then correlated with different physiological functions.

"The results were simply miraculous," he continued. "Everybody who had been receiving diksha for about one year showed a decrease in parietal lobe activity that has previously been detected only in a few highly advanced meditators with over 10,000 hours of meditation experience and in a few Zen masters and shamans. The people we tested had been doing their share of spiritual seeking before, but they were ordinary people. The stress parameters in all of them where exceptionally low. We continued to test these people as they where going through an intensive course in Golden City, and the neuro-biological restructuring kept going on with amazing efficiency. Stress patterns were reduced even more to a remarkable degree. Frontal lobe activity increased significantly and always with a slight dominance of the left frontal lobe. This is the signature pattern for healthy frontal lobe activation. If there is right frontal lobe dominance, delusions and depression can be the result, so I was glad to see that everybody receiving diksha showed a dominance of left frontal lobe activity."

From the time at age eleven when I touched my own throat and felt healing take place during a bout with strep throat, I knew without doubt that there was an energy that could have an amazing effect on the human body. Later, after becoming a priest, I could see the laying on of hands create astounding healing results. By studying the ancient teachings of Jesus and other spiritual masters, I knew this type of healing had been happening virtually forever. Obviously, it also related to the process of awakening that is known as enlightenment. Now, with this explanation of how the brain can be affected by a simple hands-on blessing, it was all making more sense.

After returning from India, I asked Christian to write an essay about all he had explained to me. Since I feel his observations are so helpful in explaining the nature of what we in the West call spiritual healing and awakening, I am including his writing titled "Comments on the Neurobiology of Awakening to Oneness" in the appendix of this book. It will give you an idea of just what goes on in our brain as we grow closer and closer to God.

The philosophy behind this transformation in consciousness reflects the timeless wisdom teachings of the East. This neurobiological blessing is designed to lead to the awakening of the true self within. In this process, the mind is seen as being so strong that, in the daily routine of life, it continually pulls us away from the present moment. We are constantly distracted, and our wandering attention is seen as the cause of all suffering. If we could only hold our attention in the present moment, we would become whole people with peace of mind and the capacity to function fully in life. Otherwise, we are experiencing the obsessive unhappiness that is characteristic of the wandering, unfocused mind. Therefore, the mind must be de-clutched and relaxed.

Instantaneously with this de-clutching, our senses heighten and the soul becomes the new command center of the human being, replacing the mind. At this point, each moment of one's life suddenly can be experienced fully. This results in the enduring presence of joy and the bliss, the birthright of each of us and the condition in which we can function as fully developed human beings. To extend this approach to life, our purpose becomes to achieve ever more advanced states of consciousness. Witnessing this effective manifestation of our shared spiritual philosophy, Celebrating Life Ministries has welcomed the Oneness Movement of Sri Bhagavan and Sri Amma as an international partner in spreading the light of transcendence. We both see such alignments as essential and necessary for humanity to take the next steps into realizing its potential for healing itself and its environment.

Hearing Bhagavan and Christian Opitz speak of the neurobiological process of diksha delivering our human birthright in the form of an adjustment in the lobes of the brain, I now could understand that the oneness of all humanity must be reflected in the wholeness of each individual human. Further, this individual wholeness is possible only through a healing that reaches in and touches the very being, the indwelling core of that person. This is true healing.

The urgency I felt on first hearing Bhagavan's name now had become obvious. The need for this type of work to succeed is overwhelming. If we don't implement powerful alternative approaches for the problems of our planet and do it soon, we're in deep trouble. Not just as individuals, but as a species. The global threats of our human-made and natural crises are of such magnitude that every possible effort must be brought forth at this time. It is urgent that healing efforts such as the Oneness Movement be moved to the front burners of concerned human beings everywhere on the planet.

But please understand. No one involved in this movement, neither Bhagavan nor I nor anyone else, is saying that the Oneness Movement is the sole human activity necessary to move our species and the world itself forward into a more enlightened existence. Attaining this condition of union with God and liberation from self-concern is the goal of all authentic spiritual disciplines. There are many approaches to moving forward, from activism for social change to the simple but profound power of authentic prayer or silent meditation or chanting of mantras. Chanting moves energy, and the sacred syllables of individual mantras send out a powerful vibration into the universe, causing our individual beings to vibrate with that resonance.

The Sanskrit mantra *sat-chit-ananda* is one such chant. Probably eight months before hearing Bhagavan's name in the night, I began studying and chanting sat-chit-ananda, for no particular reason other than I'd heard it many times and found it moving. The three words are translated from the Sanskrit as "being-consciousness-bliss." These are considered the three aspects of God when we look at the Divine from the viewpoint of an energetic paradigm. First we experience being in order to have existence. Then we take on consciousness in human form. Finally, we evolve into a state of bliss as the goal of our spiritual journey. I had been told the story that Joseph Campbell was given this particular mantra to practice during his own journey to India many years ago. Campbell said that he didn't think he could ever master completely the concepts of being and consciousness, but he certainly understood the pursuit of bliss. Therefore, he concentrated on the third Sanskrit term, ananda, or bliss. From his meditations, there emerged his personal motto that has evolved into a profound and popular byword in contemporary spiritual studies: "Follow your bliss."

Many mantras include the syllables sat-chit-ananda, and it sometimes stands alone as an individual chant. Indian teachers usually give a particular mantra to their followers as a way to stay in spiritual contact when not in one another's physical presence. Though I didn't know it when I began chanting sat-chit-ananda, by the end of my visit with Bhagavan, these Sanskrit syllables would take on a special significance.

During my time in the Golden City, I experienced numerous shifts in consciousness during various rituals and ceremonies. All were meaningful, but my most profound moment came on our final day there. When Sri Bhagavan initiates a spiritual teacher into his pathway, he practices the ancient tradition of bestowing a new name on that teacher. After the dasas performed a very beautiful ceremony, Bhagavan positioned himself in front of me and placed his hands on my head. He maintained this position for three minutes, and a vast flow of energy penetrated every cell of my body. It was like nothing I had experienced before. I burned. Profound feelings surged through me. This was his deepest and most meaningful blessing for me, a total restoration and empowerment for my return to my work in the world.

The touch of his hands was such that I will feel it forever. Then, after gently removing his fingers from my head, he looked in my eyes and said:

"I now give you your new name. You are Sri Sat-Chit-Ananda."

And I knew the truth had found me.

Meditation

Being Consciousness Bliss

Prepare for this meditation by getting comfortable, relaxing and breathing deeply. Begin by chanting the following three times, either aloud or silently:

Om Sat-Chit-Ananda Om.

The Sanskrit syllables will overlap, so that your wording sounds something like: "Saaachitaaanda."

Be silent and reflect briefly on the basic meanings of the Sanskrit terms:

Om: The primordial sound of creation. This, of course, is the ancient sound chanted either by itself or at the start or end of many mantras in the East.

Sat Chit Ananda: Being Consciousness Bliss, the three attributes of God.

Om: Creation continues.

Chant the phrase three times, then allow yourself to go deep into a contemplative mindset. Realize that the three stages of existence, being and consciousness and bliss, reflect the three attributes of Divinity. Then also realize they are the attributes of humanity. When fully present, we are in a state of being; when fully awake, we are in a state of consciousness; when fully whole, we are in a state of bliss. Realize that if we wish to heal, we can seek this state of bliss. A wonderful way to initiate that seeking is to breathe deeply and chant again:

Om Sat-Chit-Ananda Om.

Chant either silently or aloud for as long as you wish. You will know when you are finished.

◆   ◆   ◆

3

Hallowing Out a Space

I do not teach techniques of healing. I teach only one thing and that is how to connect to God. My educational model is ancient, starting with authentic prayer in order to hallow out a space within our beings into which we invite the Divine. As the sacred light merges into us, it becomes an active presence in our lives and actually performs whatever work we are called to do. In this way, we individual human beings transcend who we think we are, and we rise above the limitations of our separate individual existences.

This process brings about realization of a new inner state of being, that which Sri Bhagavan identifies as the condition of enlightenment. I often refer to the words of Saint Paul in First Corinthians in the New Testament when he wrote of "putting on the mind of Christ." But rather than "mind," I prefer to use the term "consciousness." If we put on the consciousness of Christ, then we truly connect to the reality of the light. We actually can take on a different consciousness, a different self than was there a moment before, and we begin to function differently. The old concern with "I, me, mine" will have vanished. Bhagavan might say that the activity in the lobes of our brain has changed and therefore our consciousness is operating in a new and enlightened manner. This is the inner essence that I refer to as Christ consciousness. I see the consciousness of Christ as the very beingness of God.

In order to take in this new consciousness, we must create a space into which it can enter and dwell. This means that whatever previously occupied that space must vacate the premises. More often than not, this evicted tenant of our consciousness is nothing more than some aspect of excessive self-concern, otherwise known as the ego. Sooner or later, and sooner if we're smart, we must move past the idea that everything is about "me." However, I do not agree with some disciplines and teachers who say it is necessary to "kill the ego." The ego has a job to do. It allows us to function in the outer third-dimensional world. But still, when it comes to inner healing, the ego must yield its self-importance and allow the flow of Holy Spirit to prevail. The fire of Holy Spirit, that sacred light of healing, wants to burst through into our awareness. But its progress will remain impeded so long as we're personally obsessed with "I, me, mine."

Our concern with the ego does not always surface, as we sometimes think, in ways that make us feel superior to other people. It can be just the opposite, such as in feelings of insufficient self-esteem. This issue was something I had to deal with during my visit to the Oneness University. During our group's first gathering with Sri Bhagavan, he stated that I was, in Indian spiritual terminology, an Avatar. I suppose this sounded quite sweet to me on some levels, especially those dealing with self-importance. But in other ways, I had trouble dealing with this assertion. This concept of being an Avatar within the framework of Indian spirituality came from outside my imagination and my normal reference points. For a while, I wasn't quite sure what this meant or how to deal with it. I knew Indian Avatars were supposed to be lofty beings, even Godlike. But what was the significance of this for me? What was Bhagavan telling me? Was I still human or what?

Then the dasas who were my teachers explained that there are now many such Avatars upon the Earth, all for the purpose of bringing about a change in the planet's consciousness. So I was just one of many. That was better. And it doesn't mean they're God. If a human being were to be invested with the full light of God, the dasas explained, that human would simply incinerate. Our nervous systems are not made to withstand such voltage. Furthermore, every single human being embodies some attribute of God, to one degree or another.

The attribute of God that I could manifest, according to Bhagavan, is causeless love. "People will come into your presence and feel this love," he said. "You need do nothing other than just be present. Just sit and do nothing." The whole idea was sounding better now. I'd been waiting a long time for someone to tell me to just sit and do nothing. If this is what Bhagavan wanted of me, I could do it.

As the days passed, the notion of being someone who inspires causeless love became acceptable. As the feeling settled in, there returned to me a sense of self worth and personal confidence that I had forgotten was possible. During my teens, I actually had a positive sense of self-esteem. But then I entered my studies for the priesthood, and all at once, that self-esteem was gone. Of course, one purpose of such studies is to diminish one's preoccupation with personal interests, but this is a far different concept than the Eastern focus on liberation from the ego. In the East, when the ego is overcome, the individual eliminates reactions to outer stimuli and instead functions as a whole being in tune with the Divine. But for me as a student for the priesthood, it was my sense of wholeness as a human being that vanished. So even when I knew I was doing the work of the Divine all these years, there always had been something missing.

In India, that something returned. It was my sense of personal self worth and confidence. This sense returned not only through the various teachings and rituals, but it was ushered gently back by the extreme love and care demonstrated toward me and toward all individuals by Bhagavan, Amma, the dasas and virtually every person we came into contact with at the Oneness University. These people not only espoused the idea of causeless love, they actually practiced it. I realized that a huge difference existed between the self-esteem I had lost and the ego that causes one to obsess with me, myself and I. For me, being free of egoic concerns is really a byproduct of being totally in tune with God. And when one is in tune with God, there is nothing at all to be concerned about because sacred energy is available to help us at all times. But how do we access that energy? What's the key to this secret of the light? Where do we find this essence of all sacred teachings?

Over my years of study in the Christian tradition, I've found some of the greatest revelations of the possibilities of the light in both the Hebrew Testament, generally called the Old Testament, and the Christian Testament, which is widely known as the New Testament. Here, you will find many stories dealing with energy as the literal power of God available to human beings. It's just that these stories seldom have been considered or taught within an energy paradigm, so we don't get their full meaning when we hear them told in church. To get that full meaning requires looking beyond the surface events and accessing the deeper meaning of how sacred energy is capable of influencing our lives. This demands our opening ourselves up to God.

Looking deeply, we start to accept that the flame of the Divine burns immediately in front of us and around us, above us and below us, always ready to sweep into our beings and better our lives. We start to understand it's we humans who need to thaw our frozen stances and issue the invitation for Holy Spirit to enter our beings. This involves relaxing, letting go of whatever thoughts are filling our heads and shifting our focus in order to welcome God's essence to replace those thoughts. Whether or not we are aware of it, this is our purpose anytime we gather to pray, or sit silently in meditation, or practice a breathing or yogic discipline. We are breaking into the normal, everyday routine of continuous mentality and creating a passageway to accommodate the flow of the Divine. "Hallowing out a space" is my description of this invitation to the Holy Spirit.

This is the key to understanding these stories in terms of the ability to activate divine energy within ourselves. If we want to grow spiritually and allow the Spirit dimension to embrace us and to fill us, we must learn to envision the universe as pure energy. This vision comes only as we hallow out a space within ourselves. I remember years ago, when I first began studying the sacred wisdom literature, I read of an event that has remained with me as one of the most powerful and inspiring manifestations of this Divine energy. It's all about hallowing out a space.

In the Book of Chronicles, there is a beautiful scene involving Solomon and thousands of the Hebrew people, all gathered at the site of their new temple. They are bringing the Ark of the Covenant, their representation of the living God, into its honored resting place in the temple. When the people all are gathered together and preparing to enter the temple, Solomon begins a prayer that runs three chapters long, chapters five, six and the beginning of seven. This is a very powerful prayer of what we today would call "forgiveness." But the Jewish word for forgiveness actually means "just drop it." It literally means let go of whatever your holding onto that you can't forgive someone else for. And it means you let go because the one being harmed is not the person you can't forgive, it's you. In my own words, holding on to this kind of stuff creates holes in our souls, or what I call sacred energy leaks that result in problems with the immune system and on many levels of relationships. But we'll speak more about this later.

Then Solomon prays (and this is my paraphrasing), "When Your people forget who you are, reach out and forgive them, Oh Lord." Meaning teach us how to release, how to drop it, how to let it go and get on with our authentic life. His prayer goes on and on, verse after verse, listing all of the silly things we do that cause problems for ourselves. After naming the many ways and reasons we humans hide behind for not forgiving other people, Solomon prays, "And when you see this, Lord, release them, release them, release them." He is imploring God to release the people from the effects of all they are thinking, doing and holding onto.

We don't know if this prayer took a few hours or a whole day or even longer. But we do know that when it reached its end, through the process of release, a vacuum had been created. An empty space in the heart of all the people. The space was hallowed out. Then Solomon looked up to heaven, signifying that all was right in the universe in the Presence of God, and he prayed these words:

"Oh Lord, *Adonai,* come now and take up your resting place in this your home."

With that, the sacred fire we know as the energy of the Divine came down and literally swooshed into the temple and burned up the sacrifice there. The hundreds or perhaps thousands of people gathered were so overwhelmed by this power, as though they had put their fingers into an electric socket, that they literally fell to the ground. This sort of thing happens because, then as now, people individually are wired for just so much energy and that's it. Then this higher, more powerful energy blasted into the people who had become receptive while praying along with Solomon. A vacuum, a hallowed out space, had been created for this cleansing, purifying, healing fire to enter and restore each person. Today, we identify this level of energy as the Holy Spirit.

We are given another report of a tremendous energetic experience in the story of Pentecost. What more direct statement can there be about the nature of the descent of the Holy Spirit than in Acts 2:1–4:

> When the day of Pentecost had come, they (the Apostles) were all together in one place. And suddenly a sound came from heaven like the rush of a mighty wind, and it filled all the house where they were sitting. And there appeared to them tongues as of fire, distributed and resting on each one of them. And they were all filled with the Holy Spirit and began to speak in other tongues, as the Spirit gave them utterance.

Pentecost was about the bestowing of spiritual discernment not just for each of us as individuals, but for all humankind. This awakening is the dawning of the possibility of sustainable joy and peace in the world. The awakening of oneness.

As with the story of Solomon's prayer, the coming of the light is not used as a metaphoric reference. It is given as a report of direct experience. If we are willing to embrace this as an energetic event, it can become our own personal reference point for the possibilities of the power of Holy Spirit in our lives, no matter what spiritual tradition we follow. We then begin to see the ordinary events of our everyday lives in a different way. We suddenly recognize potential where, only a few moments before, it did not exist. As we become aware of Holy Spirit moving throughout the world, transforming as It moves, we become more alert to the possibility of movement in our own personal existence. We learn to welcome the idea that true change can happen. But we truly need to accept and to know that this kind of occurrence actually can transpire before we can have reason to start to look for it. Once we do start to look, however, it's amazing how ordinary events line themselves up to demonstrate Divine influence in our individual lives.

All of this started on Pentecost, a Jewish feast of harvest, honoring the outpouring of God's bounty. At this joyous time, Jews from all over the world came to this particular spot in Jerusalem. They gathered together, speaking different dialects and even different languages. Some people couldn't understand what other people were talking about, but they communicated through the heart. When Jesus left, his final directive to the Apostles was to come together and wait for an outpouring of grace, and it was in this environment that they assembled. What they did not yet understand was that this outpouring of grace was to be an entirely new experience and awareness of divine consciousness. This would be the consciousness in which they and we could live and through which sacred energy would surge forth to touch, restore, transform and energize lives. This would become the consciousness of ascendance.

Pentecost offers us a tremendous vision of the Divine descending after a space is hallowed out by a group of people going into a sacred space through releasing concerns of the ego. Some people like to think that Pentecost is a religion. It is not. Pentecost is a covenant, a new contract binding God, the intradimensional world of Spirit and all people, because all people are God's children. The new contract states that from this point on, you do not need anyone to speak for you. You and God now have an open line of communication. God is always ready to listen and answer.

The lesson of Pentecost is that this time now-today-is the dawning of the age of Holy Spirit. In other words, each of us is offered the return of our self-esteem and self worth, just as happened with me in India, through the power of the Holy Spirit. Through this covenant with God called Pentecost, you and I can enter into and pass through the veil into the throne room of the Divine. There, we can make contact with the world of Holy Spirit. However, to enter and pass through this veil, to take advantage of this opportunity, we must develop a deep awareness, what I call Christ consciousness. Throughout the Book of Acts in the New Testament, we find stories of ordinary people energized by the Holy Spirit, energized by their awareness that nothing, not even sickness, can defeat them. In these stories, the Apostles are working in a dimension reflecting their new knowledge, heightened awareness and raised consciousness that followed the experience of Pentecost. These also are stories demonstrating to us what is possible in this life.

The questions then come as to how was this awareness released in Jesus' early followers and how is it released in us today? That answer is spelled out by Solomon in the Book of Chronicles, and it's spelled out in the story of Pentecost as well. It's simple.

The answer is *pray, pray, pray, pray, pray, pray!*

The rub is, of course, what is prayer? What is the secret to release, to hallowing out a space, to checking the ego? What did prayer mean to the Hebrews? What was the actual act of praying? If they had been in India, the Apostles might have chanted sat-chit-ananda, but they were not in India. So what was prayer to the followers of Jesus? Well, it is not the same thing many people call prayer today, where we just babble at God and we tell God everything he already knows as if he doesn't know it.

The meaning of prayer to these ancients can be understood by examining the teachings of Jesus in his own Aramaic language. As reported in the gospels of both Matthew and Luke, Jesus was a rabbi who gave teachings. He gathered his followers and gave them an incredibly powerful outline for their communion with the Divine. We call this outline "The Lord's Prayer." Many scripture scholars believe Jesus gave that original teaching over the course of days, not just in five minutes. There was no rush and he wanted them to get it. The power of those teachings are reflected in at what happened when the Apostles came together at Pentecost and waited, probably for a number of days. It was probably like a meditation retreat. I'm sure they ate and talked and sang and shared stories, but the emphasis was on creating a connection with the Divine. There is one particular passage in Acts that reveals the secret of what Jesus taught the Apostles. If you read this story of Pentecost in the original Greek, the words don't say they were gathered together to pray or in prayer. The precise translation is that they were gathered together, "united in *The* prayer."

That prayer was what we now call the Lord's Prayer, and the key to its understanding lies in the opening phrase, which we usually recite as, "Our Father who art in heaven, hallowed be thy name." But, as I have explained in previous books and in many lectures, this is a mistaken idea about how to address the Divine because of faulty translations from Aramaic into English. In the Hebrew prayer books of that time, the people were given the name of God as "I Am." We remember the great quotation: "Be still and know that I Am."

This was the name given to Moses when he asked God, "What shall we call you?" The answer came: "Tell the people I Am sent you."

"I Am what?" you might ask.

The answer: "I Am whatever the people think they need me to be in order to have their needs met."

It's just that simple. This is a universal statement of the basic premise of authentic spirituality. This statement parallels the central concept of Hinduism when *Brahman*, the highest consciousness, states directly in that tradition's sacred literature, "I am *that.*"

Thus, the Aramaic translated as "Our Father" is actually an opening address to the I Am being. The actual spoken words would have been a litany of praise through naming, a grand and effusive expression. A celebration of I Am. In our current mode of expression, this opening of the Lord's Prayer would have come out something like: Our Father/Mother, Divine Presence, Cosmic Being, Omnipotent, All Powerful, All Knowing, Pure light, Divine Energy, Pure Oneness. This is the naming of the Divine Presence whose consciousness fills all existence, whose mind fills the whole universe. It is the opposite of our thinking that we each have our own mind or our own consciousness, separated from the pure consciousness of God. The opposite of ego. This praying of the names of God is about each of us entering into this awareness that all is one. One in light. One in energy. But we have missed all of that because we haven't been taught this effusive praise as the essence of prayer. All that has come down to us down in English is just "Our Father."

"Who art in heaven" refers to the great consciousness that surrounds us, interpenetrates us. "Our Father who art in heaven, hallowed be thy name," means: "May I be aware that every time I call upon your presence, a powerful energy event is being initiated." To speak the name of God is synonymous with chanting I Am, and we are setting the stage for an act of creativity. The phrase I Am actually is neutral in terms of what is brought into being, so the words that follow determine the nature of the energetic creation. If they are positive words, a positive force is created. If the words are negative, then the force is negative. Therefore, we have to learn to make them positive, such as "I am an emanation of the divine spirit" or "I am a healthy, robust person."

By contrast, if you say of yourself something like "I am clumsy, I am stupid, I am sick," then you are using all of this energy to create negativity. If you say, "I am sick," seventy trillion cells of your body repeat in chorus, "Yeah, let's create sickness." That's why Jesus told us to watch what we say. Listen to what you say in connection with I Am because your words are pushed out into the universe with a force, with an energy of passion. That energy brings into being whatever is spoken.

If you think of the I Am essence in this way, all of a sudden you see a significant shift in the way you look at things, at people, at yourself. The inner chatter of the mind lessens. You realize that breath of life at the center of your being is with you at all times. That Presence is always there. That sacred energy is what you release every time you say I Am. The more we understand this, the more our discernment expands because we are learning to make our home in the breath, in the energy of the Divine.

Please realize, however, that this is a far different concept than using affirmations, most of which are thoughts for the head. That's not where the power lies. The power lies in that dimension we call soul, that energetic aspect of our being where the Spirit indwells. There has to be a congruency of what we think, what we speak, what we feel, what we believe and what we know. Then spirituality becomes extremely practical and fills us with joy and peace and harmony. When we live this way, even if we make mistakes, we can shift back to that paradigm of joy. We can return to that inner peace. This is what is essential.

Solomon's prayer and Pentecost are two of Christianity's most powerful statements of the potential of God's energy because they are not reported as metaphors but rather as something that really happened. They demonstrate what one must do in order to release this power that is already embedded within us. Let us appreciate what is going on here in such powerful passages in our ancient writings. This is how to read sacred literature in terms of an energy event and derive the ultimate benefit from it.

Experiencing this energetic level of power and authority is possible for every one of us. We can work toward this privately in our own silence as well as in gatherings with other like-minded people. While the effect sometimes seems to come more easily or at least more dramatically in group settings, there are many tools such as sacred literature, prayer and meditation that lead us privately into the realm of the Spirit. Even when someone has the group experience and takes home a profound healing and learning, these tools are invaluable in maintaining our focused feeling of joy, peace and healing. One unchanging attribute of reading, prayer and meditation is that these private pathways serve as access to God for both the least and most experienced seekers of divinity. As in any field of endeavor, practice yields proficiency. But none of us in these human bodies becomes so proficient in dealing with God that we no longer need to stay in touch through spiritual discipline.

The first step toward the experience of the true self and of the Holy Spirit operating in and through us is choosing to do whatever is necessary to bring this about. This may mean something like Solomon's prayer of release and letting go of a lot of stuff, changing our way of thinking and acting. Any time you go within, you may find yourself facing things in your past that are painful or humiliating or that bring up rage or fear. But you must be ready to see all that, experience it in whatever form it comes to you, and then move beyond any personal obsession or indulgence in it. In short, get over it.

Now this may sound like a tall order, to move beyond your stuff right on the spur of the moment. Granted, it may take time. It may take a great deal of prayer and meditation. You may ponder the sacred writings, you may attend spiritual gatherings, you may listen to many teachers. But somewhere along the line, if you so choose, whatever negative charge is blocking your life will release, and at that point you will know it has all been worthwhile.

On the other hand, we do have the power and the sacred permission to instantly get over whatever we need to get over, to forgive what needs to be forgiven, to release what needs to be released. So, yes, it also can happen instantly. You won't know until you make your choice to go for it. This is the essence of the Hebrew Testament's words in Deuteronomy: "I have set before you life and death, blessing and curse; therefore choose life." But you must remember, the choice is yours, and that choice repeats itself constantly, moment after moment. Now, in this very instant, is the time for all of us to realize that this is our moment of choice. So let us choose life.

Meditation

Release Release Release

In order to make oneself fully available to the fire of the Holy Spirit, or if you prefer other wording, to the power of diksha, it is necessary to hallow out a space. Feel that happening now. Sit quietly, do nothing, just be. Sit just as the people sat and listened to Solomon pray. Remember you have chosen to walk this sacred pathway, no matter what it takes.

When you are quiet and calm, allow the visualization to come to you of Solomon praying at the temple and looking down at all the Hebrew people on the grounds below him, all listening, waiting. Perhaps for hours, or even days.

Remember Solomon's words: "Lord, release them, release them, release them." Pray:

God, release me, release me, release me.

Breathe, relax. Allow yourself to let go of any emotional or mental baggage you may be carrying. Simply breathe in and then allow these feelings of emotional or mental stress to flow out of you on the outgoing breath. Let your thoughts just leave.

No matter how powerful or stressful they seem, they can and will go. You will find that it is possible for such feelings to simply vanish as you feel your heart opening.

Allow this letting-go process to take as long as it wants to take. When you begin to experience a new and different level of quiet, you will know that you have hallowed out a space.

Now hear Solomon call: "Oh Lord, *Adonai,* come now and take up your resting place in this your home."

Feel the surge of power the people of Israel felt at these words. See in your mind's eye the flame that soared through the temple, burned up the sacrifices and left the people falling to the ground. Feel this very power of the Holy Spirit firing through your own physical body. Feel it brightening your eyes and your mind.

Add to the fire by praying the invitation:

Come, Holy Spirit.

Repeat this simple invitation as many times as you wish. Notice any changes within as you continue to relax, breathe and pray.

Now become silent. Get acquainted with this feeling of hallowing out a space. Get to know the sensation of energy coming in. Get to know what Bhagavan means by diksha, what I mean by the blessing of God. Get to know the Holy Spirit.

This beautiful, sweet feeling of peace. This is your birthright.

◆   ◆   ◆

4

Shifting Away from the World

In the same century that Jesus lived, there existed an extraordinary Jewish monastic community near Lake Mareotis in Egypt, not far from Alexandria. The monks of this community practiced spiritual healing and centered their lives around nature, simplicity and devotion. They developed a culture of peace and joy in difficult times. They prayed a great deal. These monks were called the *Therapeutae*. They too have been a big part of my journey.

Monastic life, such as that of the Therapeutae, offers a unique and powerful appeal. As the ego begins to withdraw from its prominent role in our daily perception of reality, the natural result is that we turn inward. The guiding idea is that, in order to become a whole person and then to participate in the world creatively and successfully, one first must pull away internally from the distractions of the world. For these ancient Egyptian monks, that meant going away to live in a monastic community. This would be a gigantic shift for most of us, and I would imagine that such a life would be acceptable to very few in our modern Western culture. But the concept of turning away from the material world's temptations for distraction from a spirit-centered life remains valid. The world is full of magnets that tempt us to focus on them rather than the Divine, and we must reach a point where our consciousness is not drawn to magnet after magnet, moment after moment. Only then can we concentrate with reverence on sacred pursuits. But while we all do not need to enter a monastery, we can benefit from making and maintaining this shift away from the world's intoxicating distractions, even if only in our private lives or private moments. But for those precious souls of ancient Egypt, this shift meant a commitment to monasticism.

A detailed account of the Therapeutae has been preserved in the writing of Philo Judeas, the first century Jewish theologian and philosopher. In his treatise *De Vita Contemplativa,* Philo presents a finely drawn rendering of their daily life, spiritual practices and ceremonies. Noting the extent of his knowledge and his obvious affection for the monks, some scholars speculate that Philo himself was a leader of the Therapeutae. Other writers of that period confirm many of his observations of these monks in the desert, contemporaries and apparently a branch of the more widely known Essene monastic community. Philo also reports that numerous other groups of Therapeutae existed at the same time elsewhere in the ancient world, and some current scholars have theorized that perhaps John the Baptist and even Jesus himself may have been members of the Therapeutae. If Jesus was not a Therapeutae, contemporary scholars think that the Egyptian monks first may have learned of his message through the teachings of the Apostle Mark. By the third century after Jesus, other ancient historians were writing of the presence of the Therapeutae, using the name as synonymous with the Christian monks of that era.

From the writing of Philo and other records, including those of the early Macedonian ruler of Egypt known as Ptolemy I Soder, a former general in the army of Alexander the Great, we know the Therapeutae appeared in the Mediterranean world long before the time of Jesus. To find their true origins, historians turn to India. There, the historical Buddha lived about 500 BCE (or perhaps earlier, depending on what theory and research we accept). By the time the conqueror Asoka unified the Indian subcontinent through military conquest in the third century BCE, Buddhism was known as a religion of peace and harmony. Asoka, a wonderful early example of a fierce military conqueror who turned his swords into plowshares and himself into an enlightened ruler, adopted Buddhism as the state religion for India.

Throughout India, Asoka left indelible records of his military, governmental and philosophical accomplishments in carvings on large stones and slabs. Historians have discovered and preserved thirty-three of these records in rock, now known as the *Edicts of Asoka*. On these rocks, carved in the Pali language spoken by the Buddha himself, Asoka relates that he sent Buddhist missionaries into the Mediterranean world for the purpose of establishing monasteries. This was just at the time the Silk Road was being established as the great trading route between Europe and Asia, so travel between these regions had become possible and even common. Further, these stone records accurately list the names of many of the Mediterranean rulers of the time, offering evidence that there was official government contact between the two regions. Confirmation of the presence of Buddhists in Egypt at this time includes the Buddhist symbol known as the wheel of life, a distinct circle with eight spokes radiating out from a smaller inner circle, on tombstones found near Alexandria, and therefore near Lake Mareotis itself.

The Therapeutae included both men and women in equal status. Monks lived in individual houses designed for solitude within a small rural community. The natural setting was described as pleasant, and the climate mild. The Therapeutae were considered ascetics, and their communal lifestyle reflected the original meaning of their vow of poverty, that is, simply to live basically detached from the material world. They studied the Hebrew Testament and other ancient spiritual writings, including those of the founders of their order. Philo reports that the monks themselves were encouraged to write of their meditations and to compose psalms. They prayed every day at sunrise and again at sundown. Once a week and on special occasions, they gathered cheerfully in white robes to share a common meal and sing, dance, listen to teachings from a community elder. Philo writes of the blissful expressions he observed on the monks' faces during their ecstatic all-night observance of Pentecost. The highlight of that celebration featured a communal dance presentation, featuring both men and women, telling the story of Moses and Miriam at the Red Sea.

For me, the Therapeutae are important because of the feeling that comes over me when I think of them or hear about them. In other words, my spiritual discernment lets me know there's something there, a connection through which I can know myself better or do my work better. Obviously, I share many of their values and their approach to spirituality and to healing. I feel their integrity, I know they understood about hallowing out a space and moving beyond egoic concerns. They stepped away from the world to live an alternative lifestyle so that they could embody the true and deep essence of the Holy Spirit. Within this shifting away from the world, they realized their own inner shifting toward God. The philosophy of the Spirit of Peace Monastic Community, which I founded a few years ago, bears many philosophical and practical similarities to the Therapeutae, although I had no conscious thought of these ancient monks at the time of the founding. Our community prays two hours a day for world peace and also prays and meditates on the healing of the planet and all people. But perhaps more than anything else for me, the Therapeutae illustrate the balance of peace and healing created when devotion inspires a simple, natural approach to life. Practicing this approach develops our own quality of inner silence.

In Greek, *Therapeutae* is translated as "healers" or "curers." Our word "therapy" comes from this root. Some of the monks were said to have developed unusual gifts of healing. In Philo's description, the Therapeutae were said to practice a form of healing superior to the medicine of the cities, which dealt only with trying to cure the physical body. He emphasized that the healing of the Therapeutae operated on the level of the soul. On this level, the Therapeutae worked to ease the worst and seemingly incurable physical diseases, as well as a multitude of emotional problems whose origins could not be ascertained by traditional diagnosis. Today, we would refer to this work of the Therapeutae as divine healing or spiritual healing. Philo stressed that the monks' healing capacities grew out of their quiet lifestyle away from the city, living among gardens, enjoying the fresh air and peaceful atmosphere. Other writers relate that when monks of this era walked through the villages and towns, people gathered in their presence in the belief that sacred healing powers accompanied them. The people believed that all that was required to induce healing was the presence of the monks. Not even the laying on of hands was necessary.

Philo wrote that the Therapeutae had been instructed by their sacred laws to serve the living God. Their ascetic existence was chosen because the cities of that time, even those well governed, were so plagued with troubles and disturbances that they could not be endured by anyone who ever had lived under the guidance of wisdom. In their studies, the monks studied and debated sacred writings, always considering the allegorical meanings of the literature. In other words, the Therapeutae sought the mystical, energetic meanings of sacred writings. They would have understood, for instance, the energetic power attributed to Solomon's prayer for the temple as an actual power, available to all human beings and observable in third dimensional reality.

True mystics, the monks also received their own whispered messages from the Divine. They always remember God, Philo wrote, so that they recognized every happening and the content of their dreams as communication from God. He reported that they often spoke while in altered states, and such speaking was considered revelatory in terms of their understanding of their sacred philosophy.

From these writings about the ancient monks of the time of Jesus emerges our Western model for monastic life, down to the present day. Again, I am not suggesting that everyone abandon their daily activities and retreat into monasteries. That makes no sense in our everyday world of families and responsibilities. But the point is that an alternative way of living existed two thousand years ago, and we still have access to that alternative today. That access exists because simplicity and devotion were the foundation of this alternative lifestyle, and those qualities are still very much available as choices to each of us. We are capable of cleansing our lives of unnecessary, negative attachments and obsessions, and instead, focusing with consistency on the Divine. Thus, we find ourselves hallowing out a space for the Spirit to enter and embracing the true alternative to reactions to news reports of troop deployments and the most recent terrorist acts. Furthermore, this is not an alternative that weakens us or removes us from our daily activities or responsibilities. It is a choice that strengthens us and provides us the energy to move forward in a more productive, less stressful manner.

At this point, I emphasize again that I am writing with reference to my own spiritual background and tradition. I am a mystical Christian whose roots go back to the time of Jesus and the Therapeutae, and I long ago accepted Jesus as my personal teacher. I repeat this to remind you that just because I am modeling my personal belief system, I am not trying to convince anyone that this is the only way. If you come from a different tradition, there will be an enlightened master of your own tradition who has spoken of healing as the loving aspect of God. All I am offering is the opportunity for you to observe how I model my teacher Jesus. Then you can go to your teacher, male or female, and however that teacher modeled God's love, do that for yourself and others. There is no suggestion here for you to switch traditions or religions. No enlightened teacher, including Jesus, came to establish a religion. The purpose of all enlightened teachers is to demonstrate how close we are to the world of Holy Spirit and to offer us a vision of our true self, so that we can drop our limiting beliefs and realize our own proximity to God.

When we feel this closeness with God, we realize that we ourselves are capable of communing with the Divine Presence. No intercessory is necessary to carry the messages back and forth. No one technique of contact is seen as the one right way. No single religion or tradition comes to mind. Rather, as we draw nearer and nearer to the Divine, we remember ourselves as energetic beings. We actually experience the knowledge that we all are created from and composed of energy. In the Book of Genesis, when God created the world, it says the first item on God's agenda of creation was the light. Remember? "Let there be light." That's not the sun, not the moon, not the stars. God called forth light, and with every creative act thereafter, the light was involved as it evolved into energy and then into matter.

This realization of the ever present light of God opens us to the potential reality of extraordinary events such as Pentecost that seemingly defy logic and stretch the envelopes of our imagination. Our desire to experience spiritual phenomena and get a glimpse of the flow of Holy Spirit driving this sacred event inspires our journeys to faraway places where others have reported these experiences. As mentioned earlier, my own spiritual journeys of recent years have taken me to Medjugorje and to John of God's healing center in Brazil, both before India.

Medjugorje is a small village in Bosnia-Herzegovina, the former Yugoslavia, where apparitions of the Blessed Virgin Mary have been reported since 1981. In the years since, millions of people of different faiths from all over the world have journeyed there to pray for healing and awakening, and also to experience the physical phenomena that occur with regularity. My own journey there would provide a major shift in my life and my ministry. Though I truly did not expect to experience any such phenomena, my system was in for a shock. After one particular prayer service, I fell to the floor and could not move. I knew that something was going on within me, but I could not say what. Thereafter, I became more open to such happenings. Other miraculous events, similar to happenings reported by others at Medjugorje, included the chains on two of my rosaries transmuting from silver to gold. I witnessed various light phenomena and the image of Christ appearing on a statue. Later, as I contemplated the meaning of these extraordinary happenings, I wrote the following for my book called *The Healing Path of Prayer:*

> ... these experiences in themselves do not change or transform one's life unless they are pondered prayerfully. In so doing, we allow the Holy Spirit to reveal the underlying truth of these events. My main purpose for going to Medjugorje was to seek God's will for my life. After much meditating on the events, which accompanied my journeys to this isolated village, some deeply disturbing revelations were given to me who would enhance the course of my life thereafter.
>
> For instance, I was informed by an inner voice that I had been too 'hard' in dealing with people who were sick and in need of help. Although the power and the healing was God's Spirit, my lack of compassion was closing the channel for me to experience the same joy people were feeling through their communion with God.
>
> I was also told that I lacked the quality of the feminine energy of God—that is, tenderness and mercy-which Mary, the Mother of Jesus, symbolized.
>
> This tenderness and mercy were evidently missing from my healing work. There was no doubt in my mind that these revelations were a true characterization of what I had become. I had been so busy with the work of the Lord that I had forgotten the Lord of the work.
>
> I eventually realized that as I meditated more on Jesus, Mary, the Holy Spirit, and the Christ consciousness, God

could mold me into an embodiment of love, mercy, tenderness, strength, and power. Recognizing God as a God of love enabled me to rise above the seeming tragedies of life into the very heart of the mother-and-father God that Jesus himself knew.

I came to see that Mary and Jesus, taken together, express the completeness of both the masculine and the feminine energy found in the "personality" of God. These events and revelations have empowered my personal life and healing work in a profoundly moving way. I am now able, through the Holy Spirit, to be a clearer channel for God's presence and power and to introduce others to their God-a Being not only of power, but of tenderness, care and mercy.

This sacred journey fueled my shifting more toward God and away from the world. As a result of experiencing phenomena firsthand and then, through contemplation, finding deep meaning, my life benefited. But it is not necessary to make long journeys in order to beckon experiences and teachings into our life. Today, perhaps more than at any time in history, we can find many such opportunities in our daily existence.

We are living at such an extraordinary and exciting time. Even if Western culture generally is witnessing a turning away from the church, we also are seeing a shifting of mass consciousness toward more wholistic, natural and therefore more sacred lifestyles. If you read just the right books and switch on just the right talk shows, we see that physicists are discussing God, medical doctors are praising prayer, and wholistic health practitioners are multiplying. It's as though the two sides of our brain have decided to kiss and make up.

For centuries, we humans in the West have been looking at ourselves as beings whose physical, mental and spiritual essences just happened to occupy a common space. We've considered these three aspects of humanity as being acquainted with one another, but not really related. Modern thinkers trace this inner split back to the 17th century French philosopher René Descartes because his writings are seen to have reduced the functioning of the human to the interaction of wheels and gears of a machine. The intimate relationships of body, mind and spirit were denied. We learned to see ourselves as a collection of separate parts rather than a miraculously interactive wholeness. In this world view, healing became a matter of isolating one malfunctioning part and repairing that part.

Today, we even distinguish two types of thinking, left-brain as logical and right-brain as intuitive. But we also realize that a mental process embracing both sides in proper balance is more desirable than being locked in either extreme. As our thinking itself evolves toward wholeness, our approach to healing has begun to reflect a more universal and dynamic view of what it means to alter the course of infirmity in the human body. With a frequency that seemingly increases by the moment, the modern medical establishment is acknowledging and validating methods of treatment that just a few years ago were considered radical and of no merit. Yoga, herbal medicinal preparations and aromatherapy have emerged as common throughout our culture. We study Eastern philosophies that speak of the all-pervading and all-powerful creative energy that we also can call Holy Spirit. More and more, the application of this universal energy for healing physical and mental difficulties is being accepted.

In truth, however, energy as the essence of healing has never really disappeared from humanity's consciousness since ancient times. I believe that we've always known of its presence. It's just that when Descartes split up the human being into unrelated portions of body, mind and soul, much of Western humanity lapsed into amnesia about the unlimited nature of this awesome all-empowering energy. We forgot how to participate personally in the incredible healing power of God.

The restoration of the understanding and practice of this power of God, the power that I identify as Holy Spirit, is my own purpose and that of Celebrating Life. This essence of enlightened spiritual healing sends the bottom-line message that God heals. We as human beings do not heal ourselves or others. God heals. So, if we want to be healed or to facilitate healing in our fellow humans, we need to get in touch with the divine light through which infirmity transforms into health. It's a quite simple concept.

Spiritual healing is the practice of empowering our full human essence with divine consciousness to such a degree that either our own or someone else's physical, mental or emotional imbalance is transformed. It's nothing new. This was the healing practice of Jesus and the healing practice of the Therapeutae. It has been the healing practice of countless other spiritual masters and their followers throughout many cultures over the centuries. We know this because the words and reports of these masters are documented in the world's spiritual literature. Still today, even in our modern, materialistic culture, this practice of divine light remains the healing pathway of the authentic mystic. It's just that we need to shift away from the world's materialistic focus in order to perceive the authenticity and power of this approach.

In order to explain further my concept of enlightened spiritual healing, let me break down my own understanding of the healing power of the Holy Spirit into a progression of three steps. For me, this is how the Therapeutae would have understood their work. These steps are (1) the experience of being, (2) faith as the energy to command and (3) the practice of the light.

The Experience of Being

Allowing ourselves to heal is about being, not doing. Allowing God to use us as vehicles to heal others also is about being, not doing.

In our culture, we are taught to try so hard at all we attempt that we eventually come to think of potential rewards as being measured by the intensity of our efforts. This carries over throughout our life. If we get sick, we become afraid and we then look at healing as a difficult task that we have to work at. It's exactly the opposite. Again, I repeat that I've always maintained from the first moments of my ministry that God heals, I do not. If I think I'm the healer, or if you think you are the one whose efforts will heal your own body, that's just an ego game. If I'm sick, I have to get myself, my ego and all my self-concern, out of the way so that God can do the job of healing that I need. Quite often, just releasing our fear of what's happening can be a huge step in healing.

The wholeness of our bodies and minds is essential if we are to negotiate daily life, yet nothing is more common in our thoughts than the fear that debilitation is lurking around the next corner. Fear for our health has become a prime motivation in our culture, a grounds for enticing us to purchase products ranging from toothpaste to insurance policies. Television advertisements push products from pills to alarm systems, all aimed at our perceived need to protect ourselves from a million imagined dangers. The whole message is that there must be something we can do, some action we can take that it will make it all better. We are programmed by modern culture into being obsessed with doing, even when we are sitting still on our sofas.

But this is not the way of realizing God, not in any authentic spiritual system. Over and over, the great spiritual literature tells us, "Be still, and know that I Am." The words may vary slightly, but not much. An authentic spiritual path offers us avenues for clearing out our obsessions, but it all starts with realizing that it's about being, not doing. We can find the power of prayer, we can discover the sweetness and rewards of meditation. Simplicity slowly but surely begins to replace confusion in our thoughts. Then we can start to do less, not more. We begin to live with less, not more. Before we know it, the programming of fear begins to drop away. We are learning to just be. In time, the programming can disappear, and we then can become clear channels for spirit.

Again, "hallowing out a space for God" means that each of us needs to find a place of inner peace, however small or large, and maintain that space so that God can enter into us. Once the light begins to infuse us, anything is possible. But it all starts with being, not doing.

Faith as the Energy to Command

Faith in God can move mountains. Faith can play a huge role in shifting our way of seeing the world and feeling the power of God. But faith, in this context, is far more than simply saying, "OK, I trust everything's going to be OK." In order to bring faith into our lives, we must actually realize the full power of God to change our lives. I often utilize in my own spiritual retreats a version of the Indian ceremony known as *darshan,* which is translated from the Sanskrit as "seeing a holy being." If you go to India, these ceremonies may involve sitting among thousands of devotees while a holy person sits on stage, sharing his or her rarified state of being with every person in attendance. When you sit in such a ceremony, look into the eyes of such beings and feel the love they share with the whole world, you begin to get a sense of what the power of God truly means.

In the ancient Vedic holy book known as the Bhagavad Gita, it is written, "If the radiance of a thousand suns were to burst at once into the sky, that would be like the splendor of the Mighty One." This is the type of realization I'm talking about. It's a realization that fills you to the bones with the "I can-ness" of God.

In the same vein, we read in Luke 11:36, "If your whole body is full of light, and no part of it is in darkness, then it will be as full of light as a lamp illuminating you with its brightness." Experiencing this illumination is the way we ourselves heal and also the way we make it available to others. Infused with this realization of light, faith becomes the energy to command. Suddenly, we find the confidence and the knowing to command our beings to awaken, our bodies to heal. When we take this attitude and knowing into our prayers, it is no longer a matter of pleading with God to do this or that for us. Rather, it is a matter of commanding our lives to conform to the wholeness and clarity of the light of God.

The Practice of the Light

We all seek the light. We all want to heal. But how many of us realize these two desires are really one? In truth, healing cannot be an end in itself or it will be lost. The goal of healing must be enlightenment. We must want the light to fill our lives. If we are to grow through our own healing, the truth we must comprehend is that there's more to life, and my healing will bring it.

Physical or mental healing provides the momentum to launch us toward enlightenment.

Of course, the term "enlightenment" has a hundred different meanings to a hundred different people, and I've previously spoken of Sri Bhagavan's definition: living the life of the senses without the interference of the mind. But enlightenment also can mean simply taking our lives lightly, as in the old proverb, "Angels fly because they take themselves lightly." For many people, however, the concept of spiritual enlightenment exists only as an abstraction or perhaps as an out-of-reach goal. At the same time, physical or mental illness or injury is felt as such a realistic and tactile condition that the idea of healing through something they consider nothing more than an abstraction becomes more a fantasy than a possibility.

But light is a reality, not an abstraction.

As we experience the beingness of God as light, we feel ourselves driven toward wholeness, a feeling of completeness and being at one with our world. Part of this wholeness is what we call "good health." When physical or mental difficulties challenge us, the vision of our own wholeness evaporates into unreality. It may remain with us as an ideal, but we are all too aware our wholeness is not a reality at the moment that we experience the challenge of an infirmity. So at these moments, what can we do?

If we are willing to accept faith as the energy to command our own healing, if we are willing to allow ourselves to be rather than to do in order to receive this healing, and if we are willing to allow the light of God to infuse us fully, we are practicing a true form of enlightenment. This practice serves the purpose of our healing, and then returns the healed being to his or her own divine path toward service to humanity.

If we as modern humans can take comparable steps to the ancient Therapeutae and shift our focus away from the material world and onto God, then we too can embody the experience of being, perceive faith as the energy to command and begin the practice of the light. Endless and beautiful lessons await us.

Meditation

Shifting into an Energetic Paradigm

Relax and breathe into your meditative state.

In the Gospel of Thomas from the Nag Hammadi Library, it is written that Jesus said, "I have cast fire upon the world, and see, I am guarding it until it blazes."

See this fire that Jesus has cast upon the world. See it burning throughout all the lands of the world. Some places, it is burning strong, flames of good size. Other places, the embers seem to be dying. In certain dark shadows, the fire can't be seen. Still, we always know that somewhere in the world, that fire is burning and we can direct our inner eyes to return to where it is burning brightest. This is the fire of the Holy Spirit. It is present now, and it will enter each of us if we only hallow out a space.

Hallowing out a space literally means to create a hollow vacuum within yourself. We do this by breathing, relaxing, releasing and reflecting on the fire. By simply commencing this practice, you already have created your vacuum. You will recognize its presence when, just for a moment, there are no words, no thoughts. Silence, only silence. Experience the presence of your hallowed out place within. Allow the ego to vacate the premises.

In the silence, allow yourself to say the simple prayer:

Come, Holy Spirit.

Now, with your eyes closed, see the sun rise up before you. It is a ball of fire. It is huge and golden. Rays emit in all direction, but you are looking straight into its center. You have no desire to look outside the sun. Its light is almost blinding, but as you look deeply into it, you realize that it is incredibly beautiful. The sun feels like home.

As you continue to breathe gently and look deeply into the sun, you notice that it is filled with vibration. It's like watching seemingly invisible rays of heat rise off a radiator. You can see the air shimmer and move. But this shimmering is within the ball of fire in front of your eyes. If you now watch the vibrations closely, you will notice they are traveling outward from the center of the light and becoming the rays that flow in every direction from the sun. This, you know, is energy.

This fire is the core of the universe, and it is the fire that Jesus ignited upon the Earth. Within this fire is the power of healing and enlightenment that is the birthright of every human being. This is the fire that can transform lives.

Now breathe in the fire. Breathe it into yourself through every pore of your body. Feel it strengthen and nourish every organ of your body, every bone, every muscle, every bit of connective tissue. Feel the systems of your body revitalizing themselves in the presence of this golden fire. Feel your concentration relaxing and enjoying itself more and more in each passing moment.

Realize that you are feeling only one thing: the energy of God rebuilding and restoring and transforming you. Take this truth into your heart. That's what you want to feel. Realize that the sacred fire that you have taken within yourself is the fire Jesus cast upon the world, and it is ready to blaze. You may wish to extend it a personal greeting and promise to nurture it.

Continue to breathe, relax and allow the light to fill you with its heat and healing.

When you are ready, pray your own prayer of gratitude for this energetic experience. You may want to speak directly to a deity of your own personal faith, to Holy Spirit, to God. You may wish to thank your personal guides from the other side. Your expression of gratitude serves to seal the fruits of this meditative experience into your energy system.

As you finish the prayer, focus for just a moment on the truth that this blazing flame of healing is the fire of world peace as well. May this flame spread like the lightning of Heaven through all of us.

◆   ◆   ◆

5

The Energetic Nature of Healing

Jesus appeared on Earth to awaken humanity's consciousness to the reality of the Holy Spirit's offering of enlightenment, healing and joy. I do not believe that the mission of Jesus was to come and die for the sins of humanity. That's a theology I never accepted even as a Roman Catholic priest. It just doesn't make sense that God would send Jesus to die a terrible death for that purpose or for any other purpose. An omnipotent, all knowing, all powerful, all wise God can find endless ways to save people and awaken in them the essence of Holy Spirit. And that is exactly what God did by allowing Jesus to teach about the Holy Spirit. Remember, the teaching of Jesus is not about a religion, not about a denomination. This teaching is about a spiritual energetic presence that brings us an abundant life and offers an overpowering antidote to fear. Saints and masters throughout history have offered this same beautiful teaching, each in his or her own words. This is Sri Bhagavan's message as well.

When Jesus left our world, he basically had begun his mission to make all people aware that they, as the Hebrew Testament said, literally are capable of realizing themselves as emanations of God. In fact, he reminded the people of his day, and this again is my paraphrasing, "Don't you recall that your own sacred writings say that that you are extensions of God? You are created of the Divine Essence. You are incarnations of the Holy Spirit. You are an outgrowth of God. You are not the Supreme Being, but you are literally the breathing energy of that Supreme Being known as *Alaha*, the one breath that breathes through every living aspect of creation. You have access to this power and I will show you how to use it to transform the world."

This awakening of the awareness of Holy Spirit in all people was the mission of Jesus, and this is the true nature of healing, both for ourselves and our planet. Obviously, this goal has not yet been accomplished. But just as obviously, it's ongoing. In all of our history, there has never been a more opportune moment to refocus on this mission than right now in the midst of the trauma of our times. We need this Spirit, this energy, but we must realize it's not only about believing, it's about a way of being. When Sri Bhagavan speaks of the diksha ritual and its effects on individuals who receive it, he does not say it's a good thing because it makes us believe something different. You will never hear him tell anyone that they should believe in him as an Avatar. Rather, the diksha has the effect of changing the way we are. There are measurable changes in the brain's activity that makes us more relaxed and more receptive to the perception of spiritual presence. This is the same effect that we seek individually through meditation. The two go hand in hand. If one receives the blessing of the diksha, one's meditation becomes more empowered.

When I began studying the teachings of Jesus in his own Aramaic language, I discovered something very powerful. To the

Aramaic-speaking people, it would have been totally foreign to place their faith in any one person. That points up a problem with statements in the scriptures that have been translated like "Put all your faith in Jesus. You must have faith in Jesus and nobody else." There was no Jew, no Aramaic speaking person who ever would have said that. They never believed that, nor did anyone in any other ancient mystical tradition, at least that I'm aware of. What they believed was that you put your faith in your underlying connection with Alaha, God, the sacred source. The ancients believed you are never separated from the creative light of God. This simply had to be the belief of Jesus as well.

In the Gospel of Thomas, Jesus addresses this issue directly in Verse 50:

> Jesus said, 'If they say to you, "Where did you come from?" say to them, "We came from the light, the place where the light came into being on its own accord and established itself and became manifest through their image.'" If they say to you, "Is it you?'" say, "We are its children, we are the elect of the Living Father. "If they ask you, "What is the sign of your father in you?" say to them, "'It is movement and repose.'"

Misperceptions about trusting in Jesus as the sole embodiment of God actually begin with misunderstanding statements of Jesus that advise trusting your inner knowing that you and all creation are connected with sacred unity. The true meaning is to concentrate on knowing that you are connected with Alaha. With God. Once you realize you and God are one, nothing shall be impossible to you. But you have to know it. You can't just believe it, because with faith there is doubt. All the time, there is doubt. But with true knowing, there is no doubt. You know that you know that you know.

Through the course of history, there have been a number of people who have come forth in this power. But for various reasons, the movements inspired by these individuals have been squashed. Sometimes, in the most severe circumstances of earlier centuries, these inspired people even have been murdered or executed. Unfortunately, because of traditions or because of the need of the human ego to be in control, people became fearful of the Holy Spirit to the extent of developing actual spiritphobia. Time and again, such feelings have put down rising movements built on the notion of the presence of the Holy Spirit. As a result, many inspirations of the Holy Spirit lost the opportunity to spread peace and healing throughout the world. Still, this presence of the spirit directly informs the original teaching of Jesus, and this teaching has survived through all the fear of all the centuries.

For the first couple hundred years after Jesus, his followers did not concentrate on the fact that Jesus lived, died and rose from the dead. All the ancient writings indicate that was not part of their consciousness. What they believed and concentrated on those first couple of centuries was that Jesus left teachings about how to live. He modeled ways to live just as all masters do. What those early followers of Jesus wanted was to learn to understand his teachings and how to model them in their own lives. Their purpose was not to believe in some "truth." Their perception of Jesus was not about doctrine.

Personally, I do believe Jesus was raised from the dead by God. I have no problem with that because of my acceptance of the nature of energetic potential and the all-powerfulness of the Holy Spirit. But I have a big problem with the idea that all you have to do is believe in Jesus and that you do not have to practice his way of life. That's insane. I don't know any world teacher even to this day, whether it was Yogananda who passed a number of years ago or Sri Bhagavan in the present or Shirdi Sai Baba of a century ago, who would teach this as a truth. The true pathway to God isn't just about believing. The teaching is *be living,* not believing. Be living these principles. You must be living in this awakened manner for the Spirit to start operating effectively in your life. Once you experience how different this feeling is from the fear generated, for example, by our mass media or by many well-meaning organized religions, you will know. You will know that you know that you know.

Down through the ages, there have been tremendous revivals that have arisen around this energetic vibration of the Holy Spirit. They appear and then they become popular because of how they make people feel. These include the famous Welsh Revival in Wales in the early 1900's, and others in the 1700's and in the 1800's in this country and all over the world. Some extraordinary people emerged in these centuries as teachers of the Holy Spirit. But in case after case, the revivals of these recent times lost their momentum and ultimately lost their power basically due to one thing. That thing is debate among the leaders over doctrine.

One such revival was the Azusa Street Revival in Los Angeles in 1906, inspired by the preaching of William Seymour, the son of former slaves. Known to his followers as "Daddy," Seymour reportedly had learned in Texas of Holy Ghost baptism, another name for the power of inducing Pentecostal exhilaration. Once Seymour began preaching in a one-time stable on Azusa Street, the phenomena known as speaking in tongues erupted among his followers. Controversy over the nature of the revival swept through Los Angeles and resulted in large interracial gatherings. People came by the thousands to the daily services over the next three years.

The revival became so popular that it spawned the Assembly of God Church and various other Pentecostal churches. But the secret of that revival was that the people involved were not teachers, they were not pastors, they were not paid ministers. They were individuals who hungered for an experience of God, the same thing the ancients hungered after. The people of that revival met in that stable on Azusa Street, and in that stable all sorts of manifestations happened. There were no dogmas, no doctrines except that God is alive, God lives and God loves. And miracle after miracle of healing, or at least those divine occurrences that we call miracles, came into being because of the people's connection with the Divine through prayer. They would pray for hours. They would sing and sing and sing. It was Pentecost all over again. But there was basically nothing in terms of doctrine to guide them.

That revival brought people to Los Angeles from all over the world. Since this was before airplanes, many people had to come by boats, some enduring a tremendously long journey of suffering. But they knew the effort was worthwhile because they could feel the presence of the Spirit, and that rendered all else in their lives secondary. Many of these travelers were reported to have experienced healings that were termed miraculous.

Azusa Street and its resulting fire around the world flourished only those three years before the arguments began between pastors of the different denominations arising out of the movement. They argued as to what constituted the proper doctrine and dogma. And just that quickly, that was the end of the revival. Azusa Street went the way of so many movements. As soon as we begin to create formulas and try to figure out how to do this work that the Holy Spirit is perfectly capable of doing without our help, we are undermining the energetic foundation that allows us to experience the Spirit. We must learn to be, rather than to do. It's one of the most basic and most important lessons at any level of spiritual understanding.

As I have already pointed out, this was a big part of my own learning in India. Healing and enlightenment just happen automatically. No effort is required. That's the beauty of it. We just sit back and allow God to break through in a very quiet way, and suddenly the divine presence moves through us and gives us strength. It's very exciting. That's why I say that now my ministry is about oneness, about enlightenment, the sacred essence through which all things manifest.

Despite its ultimate decline, the Azusa Street Revival illustrates how some of the greatest Pentecostal movements occurred and how some of the most influential spiritual teachers and healers have emerged through the centuries. Whenever you think of the personalities of people who do healing work, you have to look at their trust in the Holy Spirit. Two of my twentieth century American favorites are Aimee Semple McPherson and her student Kathryn Kuhlman. Both kept one thought in mind: let's learn to have a relationship with the Spirit of God. One thing you will notice in this work is that without a relationship with that essence of knowing that you know that you know, the profound spiritual experiences will not occur. You have to know Holy Spirit as if it is a living person. You have to know this so thoroughly that other people cannot tell where you leave off and the spirit begins, or where the spirit leaves off and you begin. That's the wholistic connection that's needed.

But again, if you look back and study these different movements that began as revivals of the Holy Spirit, you see repeatedly that it all starts to weaken when people begin to debate doctrine. The Holy Spirit does not submit to doctrines, except for one. In Biblical terms, it goes like this: "Hear O Israel, the Lord your God is one and you shall love the Lord your God with all of your heart, all of your mind, all of your soul, every aspect of your being and you shall love your neighbor in the same way you love yourself."

That's the Holy Spirit's only doctrine. Love God, love yourself, love others. In some places in Aramaic Christianity today, both overseas and in this country, there are large groups of people who still attend Orthodox Mass conducted in Aramaic. Their ministers teach the Aramaic scriptures with an emphasis on what Jesus really meant, and they have only one doctrine: "Love the Lord Your God, and love your neighbor as you love yourself." To these ministers and their congregations, the meaning of these words of Jesus is clear-this loving completes the whole law, this is all you need to do.

But you can take it from me, whether you live fifty or sixty or eighty or a hundred years or more, it takes a lifetime to learn to live that law. Furthermore, it doesn't mean you won't make mistakes. It simply means that the power and love of the Holy Spirit can set you free. It can liberate you. I have made many mistakes in my life, but I don't live in the past. In this moment now, my only concern is for the coming years that I'm on this earth and how this expression of the Holy Spirit continues to grow, so that more and more people can be helped. Every day is a growth in the perfection of the law of love. That's the healing energy. That's the healing power. The Holy Spirit is the entity of love. All other spiritual entities, including the angels, are under its tutelage. That's why the Holy Spirit is someone to get to know personally. That was the intention of Jesus for each of us.

Although the essence of the revival of Holy Spirit has appeared previously, the time is now ripe because the people are ready. Our culture is at a point of mass disillusionment because virtually nothing in our daily life leads us into a release of fear and an awareness of the transcendent presence. In spiritual terms, we have seen medicine fail us, science fail us, technology fail us, the churches and the religious institutions fail us. The governments and politicians are failing us. As good as all these things are in their specialized areas and functions, they still fail in terms of providing a spiritual feeling for life. These social institutions have themselves become the instruments of creating and perpetuating the disabling fear of our times. We know there has to be more than what we are experiencing today, so we literally have no alternative other than searching for a different way of being and living.

Let's say that we are in agreement that this is the time to choose a new way of being that recognizes the possibility of liberation and healing for ourselves and for the world as a whole. Further, let's agree that we must love God, love one another and love ourselves. Even further, let's say that we are sensing that the presence of God either already is moving in our lives or is eternally ready to do so. How do we take the next step, and the next? What is the nature of the work we must do on ourselves? How do we proceed toward our ultimate goal? Where is our freedom? This too is addressed in sacred scripture.

There is a statement from Saint Paul that I have never heard any preacher of any Christian denomination talk about. In many forms of Christianity, as we've already discussed, the general concept is that once you accept Jesus, you are saved. This gives us the idea that there is nothing else we have to do but sit there. Yet Saint Paul said, "All of us must work out our salvation with a sense of awe and trembling." I have never heard anyone preach about what that means, because you can't figure this out with a third dimensional mental approach. You have to use your spiritual discernment. If I supposedly am saved because I have accepted Jesus and I have nothing further to do such as serve others or whatever, then why does Paul say that you have to work out your own salvation? The only way this makes sense is that he is speaking from a mystical perspective, indicating that when you leave this third dimension known as the physical world, the work continues on the other side. You continue to work because you are not perfected. Your work on yourself, your work on your salvation, goes on and on because your consciousness and your awareness go on and on. It doesn't end here. Death is a transition to our next phase of being, not an extinguishing of existence.

When I reached this understanding more than twenty-five years ago, it helped alleviate a lot of my fears and feelings of being alone and separated. It may not have appeared that I felt that way because I was among lots of people almost all the time, but you can be extremely lonely in a crowd if you feel separated from the life force. So I started to look at what was wrong with me so that I eventually could go to the other side as aligned as possible with the Spirit of the Living God. I had to look at my impatience, my jealousy, my bitterness-all of these things.

Then I had to ask the help of the spirits, and I stress that in the plural. I am speaking of the individual Holy Spirits within the greater energy field of *the* Holy Spirit. Saint Paul writes in his letter to the Hebrews that we continually are surrounded by a cloud of witnesses. Is he talking about live third dimensional people? No, he's talking about the dead. The dead who have worked out their salvation in this earthly dimension and gone to the other side, beings more perfected than we are. Through this understanding and ultimately through connection with some of the wondrous beings of the other side through prayer, my own life changed dramatically.

This is the bigger picture of working on ourselves and our world, and again, this is in the nature of the original teachings of Jesus. When we talk about spirituality this way, we are talking about maintaining our awareness in an ongoing manner. We are talking about practical living that benefits the planet, benefits others and benefits ourselves. We are talking about a way of being that affects the state of being of the world. We're speaking of the roots of world peace.

Paul also made it clear that God chooses the weaker vessels of this life to confound people who think they are strong. That perception also made a great impact on me. Sometimes people say to me, and I also have heard it said to friends of mine in this line of work, "In your last incarnation, you must have been a very holy person." I laugh and say, "No, you don't understand. Doing what I do today does not mean I was holy in my last life. I just have a lot of debts to pay off this time around." My friends say the same thing. This, you see, is just another way that we keep working out our salvation, keep working toward perfection. Our whole purpose is to show through the manifestation of the world of Holy Spirit that we have opened up to this other dimension, and we allow that dimension to come through to help the people still living in this third dimension.

This acceptance of the existence of other dimensions is an essential part of living traditions around the world, including the ancient teachings of many indigenous peoples. It is the essence of Christian Spiritism, a contemporary vision of Holy Spirit that serves as a foundation for healing practices in the Philippines and in Brazil. In recent years, I have made three journeys to Brazil to visit my spiritual brother João de Teixeria de Faria, internationally known as John of God. Extraordinary healings are manifested there through the numerous spiritual entities that work through João. People by the hundreds and thousands journey from around the world to his healing center, the Casa de Dom Ignacio. Experiencing firsthand the tremendous potential for healing that exists in this system of understanding moved me profoundly.

Communing with other realms of existence also serves a backdrop for understanding the teachings of Jesus far differently than through institutionalized religion. People sometimes ask, "This idea about Jesus being a teacher of the Holy Spirit is something new, isn't it?" Well, only if you consider a 2,000-year-old idea as new. The whole focus of the early followers after Jesus and the Apostles left was to make the world aware of the existence and potential of Holy Spirit. But in Christianity, that's become the lost art. As a culture, our religious practices haven't truly recognized the Holy Spirit or the individual Holy Spirits for at least a good 1,500 years. And when that recognition has surfaced at times, it has faced either eradication through the violence of spiritphobia or submersion into a concentration on doctrine rather than experience.

Every now and then as the centuries pass by, of course, along comes a Saint Francis or a Hildegard of Bingen who recognizes that, "Wait a minute. This spirit world is very real and I would have far fewer problems if I would learn to connect." Often these people would be on their deathbed, dying physically, when the realization came. Then they got off that deathbed and, for the most part, they were never sick again. Then they tapped into the spirit world and used it for their teachings and revelations.

For Hildegard, the 12th century Benedictine abbess in Germany, her realization of Holy Spirit produced an incredible array of artistry, paintings, symphonies, poems, techniques for healing and more. Her work was all encompassing. It's amazing that all that grace existed in one person. Or did it? Was it all in one person, or did one person learn to tap into the many Holy Spirits within the Holy Spirit and allow them to come through? Maybe a particular spirit who was very artistic came through and taught her to paint sacred paintings. Maybe another came through to teach her to write symphonies. Another to teach her how to utilize herbs and crystals for healing. And another came through to show her how to lay hands on the sick and heal them that way. I mean, this woman encompassed the whole gamut. But how did it start for her? Hildegard's own writing relates it this way in her first book *Scivias* (in Latin, short for *"Scito vias Domini,"* meaning "Know the ways of the Lord"):

> When I was forty-two years and seven months old, a burning light of tremendous brightness coming from heaven poured into my entire mind. Like a flame that does not burn but enkindles, it enflamed my whole heart and breast, just like the sun that warms an object with its rays ... A voice from heaven was saying, 'O weak person, you who are ash of ash and decaying of decaying, speak and write what you see and hear. Since you are timid about speaking, and simple in your explanation, and unskilled in writing about these things, speak and write ... as one who hears and

understands the words of a teacher and explains them in her own way.'

This was Hildegard's own direct experience of healing, and she lived and celebrated the Spirit for nearly another forty years. So why do we today think such experiences and feats are beyond us and not available to us? Or even if we do trust in God and that such things are possible, why does this not work for us?

My belief is that spirituality doesn't work for a lot of people because they have not been taught to view spirituality from an energy paradigm. We in the West tend to be so analytical. We overthink almost everything. It's easy and convenient to break everything down in analysis and to create definitions that then become beliefs. We deconstruct our perceptions and then become so fascinated with the result of the deconstruction that we forget about our original perceptions. We end up not seeing the vibrancy of the wholism of life. But the truth is that all of creation is energy. This is what we are told today by modern science, but the Hindus and ancient Persians had this teaching thousands of years ago. Spirit is energy. Breath is energy. Thought is energy. The body is an energy system made up of many smaller energy systems. How can anyone think it is possible to connect with this energetically pure being of God from a non-energetic viewpoint?

Just to assure you that we are all in this together, I have made this same mistake more than once. There have been times when I have ignored the paradigm of life as energy, when I put my focus on the mental and the intellectual. But I have learned that what really makes the difference in life is experience, not theory. And the only place you get the experience of energy is in the experience of energy. For instance, you can't just read about it as you would read a novel for entertainment. You just can't read a book about the energy of Holy Spirit and say, "Oh that was really good," and stop there. Your reading may have fed your mind and your brain, but you didn't feed your soul. You didn't feed the spirit, the essence of God within, this fire that needs to grow in order to awaken the true self. This feeding of the soul is what healing is all about, and it comes only through the experience of God.

In order to experience this type of healing, we must commit to do whatever is necessary to create change. Further, we know that we must begin to perceive life through an energetic paradigm if we want our spirituality to work. This opens us to see the teachings of Jesus and other masters as dynamic guidance rather than institutional dogma. It also allows you, the individual spiritual seeker, to travel new pathways in order to discover answers to the perplexing questions of life. By experiencing the energetic nature of sacred writings and meditative practices, every person can be filled and moved by the actual feeling of the Holy Spirit.

Experiencing this feeling is one purpose of the meditations in this book. When you make a clear choice to do whatever is necessary to awaken your true self and perceive God and Holy Spirit in your life, any questions you have about your pathway start to disappear. You simply begin to know. As you continue personal study and prayer, you will learn to trust that knowing. I explain often that I teach only that which I have experienced personally. No theory, just experience. The emergence of Holy Spirit for me has been my own definite experience, the most important of my life. Once you feel this energy, you will never feel alone again, in any moment of crisis or at any other time.

Meditation

Checking for Healing

This is a very brief meditation that can be practiced anywhere, anytime, and you might want to do it several times a day. The more you practice, the more effective this meditation becomes. It involves asking yourself a simple question: Am I seeing the world of God right now?

Previous meditations in this book have begun with sitting, breathing, relaxing and reflecting. To prepare for this practice, simply stop in the middle of whatever you happen to doing at any given moment during you day, whether you are working, talking, whatever. Make sure, of course, that you're not creating a difficult situation for yourself or anyone around you. Like, maybe don't do it while driving seventy miles an hour down the freeway.

To start, merely take a deep breath or two, then breathe normally. Ask yourself:

Am I seeing God right now?

Let the response come directly and honestly. Do not try to affect the answer. If the world you are seeing is positive, full of attractive perceptions, love, hope and trust, if you feel that true peace on earth is possible, then your perception is quite simply the world of God. You know that your true self is present. That's great. Hold your focus and live on.

If, on the other hand, you catch yourself perceiving a world filled with negative images or thoughts, you will recognize it instantly. You easily can identify your inner reactions such as fear, hatred, repulsion, jealousy and anger to whatever is happening in your life. If we are filled with expectations of the people and situations in our life, then we will be making comparisons and judgments about them. That will result in some things being considered good and other things bad. This is a mindset of duality. It's not the world of God. But for many of us, as we start this meditation, we will find ourselves in this world of duality. If so, the next step is the simple prayer:

Come, Holy Spirit.

Say your prayer with full devotion. Then repeat it as many times as it takes until you actually feel something changing in your heart and mind. If necessary, review the process of previous mediations and allow yourself to experience the release of Solomon's prayer and the hallowing out of a personal space within yourself for God's essence to enter. Look for something in yourself as an indicator of a change of being: perhaps a little smile, a sudden relaxation, a straightening of the spine, whatever. Even if you don't feel anything, something is happening. In time, you'll get the feeling.

Breathe, relax and send gratitude to the deity or other Holy Spirit of your choice.

Resume your daily activity.

Repeat as often as you want, hour to hour, day to day.

If you prefer, substitute the Sanskrit mantra, "Om Sat Chit Ananda Om" that we worked with in an earlier meditation. Or use any other mantra or simple prayer that works for you. This brief meditation may take only a few moments, but its impact can be great. In time, you will realize that God is always there, the opportunity for peace is always there, and the pull of negativity never has to be there. It's just a matter of seeing God in all things.

◆   ◆   ◆

6

The Art of Devotion

Practicing devotion allows each of us to hold ourselves constantly ready to embrace the light. This is the purpose of Saint Paul's oft-quoted directive from his first epistle to the Thessalonians to "pray without ceasing." He's not talking about walking around twenty-four hours a day with our hands in prayer position and mumbling words about our needs. Unceasing prayer is about a state of mind, a focus, a way of seeing the world and relating to its happenings around us. It's about seeing God in all things. Reaching this constant condition is the purpose of the art of devotion.

Devotion is what Paramahansa Yogananda spoke of as he described his own focus, both waking and sleeping, in his classic poem "God! God! God!" in the book *Whispers from Eternity:* "From the depths of slumber, As I ascend the spiral stairways of wakefulness, I will whisper: God! God! God!"

Many years before Yogananda, the revered 19th century Indian teacher Ramalinga composed an epic poem called *Jothi Agaval* (Grace Light), in which he taught that ardent devotion to God was necessary to develop one's connection to the light. One central verse is translated as: "You will reach the Divinity if you try very hard to do it! Pray, meditate and have devotion to

God. Thus all the veils that had been [obscuring] the true knowledge will fall."

One reason that Ramalinga is held in high esteem in India today is because of his followers' report that he vanished into light in 1874, a story still told. But another reason is his extensive poetic explanation of the nature and workings of light itself within and around the physical body. He wrote:

> By the grace of God, through communion and devotion to God, matter is converted into energy. The atoms of the elements, which constitute the body, are alchemised into pure and perfect atoms resulting in a body of love. In short, matter is converted into energy. Then the body will again be transformed into a body of grace and light. By further concentration (devotion to God and deeper meditation), the body of grace and light will be transformed into the body of wisdom, eventually to evolve into the body of the God Supreme or Immanence Within.

Ramalinga is considered to be a forerunner of Sri Aurobindo, the 20th century sage. Aurobindo spoke of a coming "Supramental Descent," an awakening of humanity to a more enlightened and powerful way of living. Some current writers see the work of Sri Bhagavan and Sri Amma as one manifestation of Aurobindo's vision. In 1963, 13 years after his passing, Aurobindo's spiritual partner who was known simply as The Mother created the international community known as Auroville in southern Indian, based on his principles. In the words of The Mother, the former French mystic and artist Mirra Alfassa, "Auroville wants to be a universal town where men and women of all countries are able to live in peace and progressive harmony above all creeds, all politics and all nationalities. The purpose of Auroville is to realise human unity."

Throughout all these writings, however, we find concentration on the principle that the individual human will heal first and then work to spread that healing light throughout the world. Ramalinga's writing asserts that, through the light itself, the most impure physical body can be transformed into purity. This transformation, he said, is possible through a "principle of light" that embraces two components: compassion toward all beings and devotional meditation. Ramalinga's best known words come from his "Prayer for the World":

> Divine Lord, in the dark night you awake me to give your light. You entered and occupied my heart; your bliss is ineffable. Permit that the entire world reach this Supreme Happiness just as I have obtained it. This is my request.

In my own view, sincerity in devotion is the most overlooked yet essential aspect of healing because it is the divine ingredient that readies us to embody the Holy Spirit fully and creatively. To bring this statement down to earth in popular terminology, we can say that it behooves us greatly to develop an attitude of gratitude. But I also want to emphasize that my viewpoint has arisen through my own experience, not solely through reading the beautiful words of others. Virtually all these ideas that have come forth to guide me over the years stem from my personal guidance. As I explain in my writings and public speaking, there is no substitute for personal experience in communing with God. It is through such experience that we develop our ability to discern what messages come to us through the light and which come simply from our own ego.

So how do we develop our art of devotion, how do we encourage God to link us up with this type of guidance? I think of it this way. In the stillness of our deepest beings, we know a truth beyond anything that we can think or feel. We know that a central, primordial force of unimaginable intelligence exists. We may identify this incredible essence as God or Great Spirit or Allah or Sacred Mother. Our words, though they vary from one tradition to another, do not alter the nature of this wonderful presence.

As each of us individually tunes into God, the very core of our existence comes alive. The more we connect, in terms of both time and intimacy, the greater the reward. We become filled with unconditional love and joy. Our health and relationships improve. Our daily existence in the material world may change in unforeseen ways. Our total being takes a quantum leap toward wholeness. We become better people. We'd like to stay in this state of being all the time.

But we also know that our everyday world offers a drastically different version of existence. A dramatic inconsistency exists between our culture of fear and the devotional teachings of the great masters. While fear runs rampant everywhere in our daily culture, we find consistent statements throughout the world's sacred writings that we should not be afraid. In the First Epistle of Peter in the New Testament, we find, "But even if you should suffer for what is right, you are blessed. Do not fear what they fear; do not be frightened."

Again, this sacred teaching-do not be afraid. And again, how do we bridge the distance between the very real fear we feel and the inner peace we know is necessary not only for our own healing but also for the healing of the whole world?

We can do it with devotion. We initiate construction of this bridge on which light can travel between peace and fear and overcome the fear. Then as we center within our own hearts, find God and truly know God, our next natural act is to reach out to other people with this same light. When we do this, Holy Spirit acts through us and our fear vanishes. Our hearts and minds are filled with sacred purpose instead of fear, expectations and judgments. There comes an actual change in our inner being. We can feel it. This is what it means to find God in our daily lives. Another obvious benefit of letting go of fear-based considerations is that we will be moving toward personal healing as well.

Devotion is what the Therapeutae practiced in putting all their attention on God. Their lifestyle, their meditation and their celebrations were focused on the Divine. Within the framework of devotion, intention obviously is important, as are faith and trust and confidence. But while almost no one ever states that the main ingredient for prayer and spiritual work is devotion, it absolutely is the key.

There is a passage in the sixth chapter of the Book of Acts, in which the deacons of a church get into a big argument. There are certain women complaining they are not getting enough food and the others are saying yes you are. This fight is going on because they are human. Even in a spiritual community, people will argue over the world of matter. So the deacons come in and say, "Look, we are going to choose some highly spiritual beings among us who are going to listen to the two sides. They are going to counsel together and get the word of God to help these people so we don't keep running into these problems." Then they go on to say, "While this counseling is going on, most important of all, the rest of us will devote ourselves to prayer and the word." When you read this passage in the original Greek, the concept denoted by the word "devote" projects the idea of the word given to the individual by God.

Unfortunately, there have been Christian versions of this passage that have translated "word" as meaning "the Holy Bible." But the Bible had not yet been written, so that interpretation is ridiculous. We are left facing the question of what is this energy of devotion to the word?

Quite simply, "word" refers to the fallout of authentic prayer, the wisdom that comes through our listening within the stillness of the silence. This means receiving a personal word on what you can do to transform yourself, heal yourself, restore yourself and help others. The deacons' guidance had nothing to do with the sacred book called the Bible. They were declaring that their full attention would be given to connecting with the Divine and listening to the guidance. Further, they knew that this devotion also would bring them the courage to step out and apply that guidance. If there were not immediate results, they didn't worry because they had heard Saint Paul say, "All things work together for good, for those who are devoted to God."

These people understood that sacred energy both enters us and is released within us through devotion. In India, the spiritual teachers talk a lot about devotion. Here in the West, we don't hear that and we seldom have experiences of devotion. A lot of our church services and other supposedly sacred services are very much non-devotional. Devotion means our whole heart, our whole guidance and focus is on the Divine and the attributes of the Divine. We dwell on that in order to become that again. This is how we find our authentic selves, because we actually were this type of energy when we first stepped into this life.

The simple way of describing this process is to say that we must devote ourselves to prayer and to listening to that very still voice within, that still voice of the Divine that never shouts or screams. This is the voice the Therapeutae heard in the night and that we can still hear today.

It's as Elijah said, "I went up to talk to God and I was on the top of the mountain, and I found that God was not in the thunder, God was not in the wind, God was not in the cyclone. I found God in the small whisper." The sound of God's voice isn't about shouting, and it isn't about noise. It's about taking a deep breath and then, in the silence that arises, simply listening.

If we practice this type of devotion daily, our world begins to change. Even if we watch news reports of atrocities, even if we find ourselves staring at commercials for products we don't need or want, the projections of those presentations will not shake us internally or shape our thinking as they did previously. A passage from the British poet William Blake declares, "If the doors of perception were cleansed, everything would appear as it is, infinite." The more we are tuned to the presence of the infinite, the less susceptible we are to the fearful environment that our material world tries to project around us.

But as we progress in our capacity and commitment to devotion, we must always keep our discernment sharpened and alert. Gandhi wrote, "The golden rule is to test everything in the light of reason and experience, no matter from where it comes." So the question arises, are we just sticking our heads in the sand and assuming the mantle of devoutness while actually avoiding reality? And the answer is-no, we are not. Even our most advanced scientific thinkers now are looking at the world through a window of perception that acknowledges the energetic nature of reality.

One of the benefits of living in our modern age is that evidence is available through science and technology that the ancient teachings on spirituality and manifestation are based on realistic concepts in terms of physical existence. Quantum mechanics, a field of study that has risen to prominence in just the past century, has demonstrated many ideas about energy consistent with ancient philosophy. This field of scientific investigation has yielded a vision of our most basic reality as tiny, sub-microscopic particles and waves interacting in ways that do not conform to third-dimensional understanding of material reality. Quantum mechanics suggests that what we see is not necessarily what exists. Rather, the world can be viewed scientifically as an energetic construct that can be altered dramatically by influences invisible to our human eyes. Influences such as prayer. And devotion.

Such a vision undercuts our Western culture's deeply imbedded acceptance of duality as the foundation of the material world. Once we accept that distinctions such as solid and fluid or visible and invisible are not absolute opposites but rather descriptions of one essence in different states of existence, we also start to question the validity of the ultimate philosophical distinction, that of good versus evil. If we are going to base our reality in simplicity and devotion, this is a concept that we need to grasp fully in order to release ourselves from its influence.

There are statements about spiritual concepts that have been taken metaphorically in Christian circles for many centuries because, as with most sacred wisdom literature, the mysticism behind the terminology has never been understood. The concept of sacred light existing concurrently with darkness is not real. The creation story directly addresses the unreality of this duality. When God spoke to Adam and Eve, he said, "You can eat of any fruit. You can partake in any of the energies of the garden except one tree, that tree which is the knowledge of good and evil." In other words, the beginning of the end occurs when we begin to give equal weight to the realities of good and evil, light and darkness. The meaning of the sacred writings is that all that truly exists is good. We can think of it accurately as good, more good, or less good, but not as evil. All there is is light. More light, less light, but no darkness. Through devotional practice, this concept becomes our actual experience.

When God was talking to Adam and Eve, He was talking to all of us. This wonderful God called by many names was saying the beginning of all problems occur when we begin to believe in the simultaneous reality of good and evil, darkness and light. Once we begin to believe in this duality, an energy system called "versus" comes into existence. Light versus darkness. Good versus evil. Us versus them. God's with us against them. It's amazing but true that the vast majority of wars in history have started over religious doctrine and dogma. For millennia, people have used God as the reason for going to war. Presidents of this country and leaders of other countries still declare boldly that "God is on our side." Both the Crusades and the Inquisition of the Roman Catholic Church were prime examples of events brought about by the duality of good versus evil.

The question that arises in my mind and heart is who determines who is good? Who determines who is evil? God said to eat all of the fruit, to partake of all of the energies, except for that energy emanating from the tree of knowing good and evil. He was saying, "Don't buy into that distinction because there is no such thing, and if you start thinking that way, you're plunging into unreality." The outcome of this plunging is being lost in fantasy. If that fantasy becomes embraced by someone with control over people, terrible danger lies ahead.

Taking this to a personal level, the moment we began to realize that the mind of God embraces only health, we begin to heal. As we come to accept that there is health, more health or less health, but in the mind of God there is no illness, then illness ceases to exist. Illness is not a part of the persona of God. As we accept this realization, our true self continues to emerge.

When Jesus said, "Judge not by appearance," he was talking about the judgments we make based on duality and the three-dimensional five senses. His message was that these appearances are deceiving because they are based on non-reality. In the eyes of the Divine, there is no room for this fantasy of duality, of darkness existing alongside light. When we are fully devoted to God, this is what we know. Conversely, whenever this wholeness registers as our perception of the world, we are practicing devotion.

If every one of us human beings, for one split second today, could give up his or her belief in duality, there would be an instant transformation on the face of the planet. But that will not happen until each individual commits consciously to develop the spiritual self so that each of us becomes the light of the world. When we become the light, we model that light. We do not model darkness. Yes, we do make mistakes. But I repeatedly say that even though you may fail at something, never call yourself a failure. You are not a failure. An infinite being cannot be a failure. You are a spiritual being moving steadily toward the light, no matter how things may appear to your human eyes in a given moment.

As we accept this reality, seeing ourselves as spirit and extensions of the Divine light, our lives begin to change. Our own light brightens, and the idea that we are light transforms from metaphor into reality. In the beginning God said, "Let there be light," an energy emanating from God's own consciousness, God's own spirit, God's own compassion, God's own tenderness, God's own love. This is the real world, and every vibration of light that emitted from the words "let there be" were emanated from the creative energy of the Creator.

When I focus on those words "let there be light," as I have for some forty years, relating these statements to the creation story and to light gives me the hope and courage and strength to keep seeing the light in myself shining brighter and brighter. It also strengthens me to make the commitment that, no matter what happens between you and me or between others and us, we must penetrate that illusionary wall of perception that says this, that or the other are darkness personified. To see the light in yourself will assist you in seeing the light in others. That's what's essential. We are all children of the light.

Let us always remember, in the spirit of the master teachers of the ages, non-duality is the ultimate simplicity. The essence of devotion. Even if we cannot live in a desert monastery, we can hold this perception of God in our minds and hearts as part of our ongoing devotion.

This teaching is in full alignment with our earlier consideration of the spiritual philosophy of Sri Aurobindo, who described the Supramentality that humanity is experiencing as it evolves into a new stage of being. Writing in the early twentieth century, Aurobindo saw the destiny of humanity ready to evolve into a higher state. This evolution involved the descent of a higher form of consciousness from the spiritual realm of existence to the physical realm, infusing the physicality of humanity right down to the cellular level. One aspect of this life-changing transformation is the nature of our perception of existence. As we grow beyond the seemingly constant temptation to see the world in terms of duality such as good and bad, we would move into a condition of wholeness. Devotion would become our natural state.

One aspect of this life-changing new mentality is the nature of our perception of evolution. "Nature shall live to manifest a secret God," Aurobindo wrote. "The Spirit shall take up the human play, this earthly life will become the life divine." In essence, we would become able always to see the good in everything and our obsession with duality would vanish. Aurobindo's writings on this vision of the enlightenment of humanity continue to influence many spiritual movements in India and around the world.

Chanting the names of God can become a powerful devotional practice and one passageway into this vision. Known universally by the Sanskrit term *Namasmarana*, this practice comes soaring to us from across the board in ancient religions and spiritual traditions. In the words of contemporary Indian holy man Sathya Sai Baba, "Let the mind wander as it likes. Do Namasmarana. It is like placing the pot of water on fire for boiling. The fire of Namasmarana eliminates all the impurities in mind and it becomes pure. That is the secret."

Chanting the names of God uplifts our consciousness and attunes us to a vibrational level where we touch the Divine. I personally have practiced and taught Namasmarana for many years, and I can attest firsthand to its power for bringing peace to the mind and restoring calmness to the heart. But my experience is merely one person's testimony reflecting the directives found in sacred literature from so many times and lands.

"The Name of God, if recited with love and faith, has the power to bring upon the eager aspirant the Grace of God," Sathya Sai Baba has been quoted. "The Name has the overmastering power of even leaping over the ocean. It can award unimagined strength and courage."

"Contemplate solely the Name of God," advises the Sikh holy book *Sri Guru Granth Sahib*. "Fruitless are all other rituals." Elsewhere in this sacred writing, we find, "Enshrine the Lord's Name within your heart. The Word of the Guru's Bani (wisdom) prevails throughout the world; through this Bani, the Lord's Name is obtained." From Guru Arjan Dev, another Sikh master, comes this guidance: "All the sources of creation, and all languages meditate on Him, forever and ever."

Another approach to Namasmarana is to chant names of the attributes of God. For instance, *Rapha* in Hebrew means "God is my health." Obviously, chanting Rapha would be a meditation for physical healing.

In Islam, we find a particular emphasis on naming the attributes of God. The Koran reveals ninety-nine names of attributes of the light such as the Merciful, the Master, the Generous, the Truth, the Compassionate and so on. During the holy days known as *Ramadan*, many Muslims meditate on a different aspect each day in order to learn to see Divinity in every situation of life.

One of the most common names for God in Islam is *Rahim,* meaning the Merciful, often used in everyday devotions by Muslims. Rahim also is chanted as a meditative opening for certain ancient Persian rituals. Persian linguists have observed that "Ra-him" can be taken as a combination of "Ra," the ancient Divine Being usually associated with Egypt, plus a derivative version of "Om," the Sanskrit sound of creation. Seen in this way, this name of God represents a resolution of duality, indicating that the being of God and the act of creation are of one essence. This corresponds to the observation of contemporary science that the light beam projects qualities of both particles and waves. In other words, the Supreme Being is both the doer and the doing.

Although the actual word chanted as the name of God in various languages obviously differs, the key to this meditation is never the particular name used. The name may refer to an ancient goddess of the home or even a modern understanding of our source such as "Evolutionary Creator." All that does not matter. As with all spiritual pursuit, the key is devotion. If we do not practice with devotion, even Namasmarana is just another form.

"When through rituals and formalities you create the spiritual space and atmosphere you are seeking, then the process will have a powerful effect on your experience," writes the Dalai Lama. "When you lack the inner dimension for that spiritual experience you are aspiring to, then rituals become mere formalities, external elaborations. In that case clearly they lose their meaning and become unnecessary customs, just a good excuse for passing time."

Developing devotion into a personal art form is about transformation, about recognizing the Divinity within yourself. This requires focus and dedication. You have to go deep to find this truth. Chanting the names of God takes our inner concentration back to earlier conditions of our existence, returning us to a state of primordial proximity to our sacred source. With proper devotion, this chant transports our awareness far beyond the limits of our intellect.

Meditation

Namasmarana

Meditating on the different names for God is akin to delving into each tradition's vision of the Divine. The various individual perceptions of God come together as pieces of the puzzle in our understanding. This enables us to form a better idea of the persona or personality of this entity we call God. No one word or even a whole plethora of words can really define God. Every definition sets a limit on something. If you attempt to define God, you are setting limits on that which is limitless. That's why chanting the various names can be more effective than study in developing a broader experience of the Divine.

Although each culture inflected the actual articulation of names of God according to its own linguistics, one commonality appears almost universally. The sound of "ah" occurs either at the beginning of the name of God, as the name itself, or at the end. The originators of these spiritual traditions recognized the sacred energy from the sound of "ah." The Egyptians used Ra, pronounced "Rah." There is Allah, and the more ancient Alaha from which Allah was derived. There is Jehova and Yaweh, among other Jewish names of God. These names all are embodiments of Divine energy, as were the human beings called Buddha, Krishna and Ishwa, the Aramaic name of Jesus.

Now that we have studied Namasmarana a bit, let us put our studies into practice with a brief warm-up recitation. Here is a partial list of the many ancient names of God, most of which we've already mentioned. In addition, Inanna was Goddess of ancient Sumeria; Astarte was a Semitic Goddess worshipped by Syrians, Palestinians, Phoenicians and Egyptians; and Ishtar was the Babylonian goddess known as the light-bringer. Rama and

Shiva are Hindu names for different aspects of the Divine Creator. One way you might want to extend your own experience of this meditation is to create a project of adding to these ancient names of God. The list can grow extensively.

Remember all the previous work we've done to hallow out a place for God and to awaken the true self. Breathe deeply a couple of times and gently go for it. Start at the top and chant each name three times, either silently or aloud.

Alaha
Adonai
Allah
Jehovah
Yaweh
Rama
Ra
Ahura
Inanna
Astarte
Ishtar
Krishna
Buddha
Yeshua
Shiva

As you recite each name with devotion, notice the feeling in your body. Even if this is new to you, you may feel a sense of stillness, of not wanting to get up from your chair but rather wanting to just stay put. This is the experience of authentic prayer and meditation. With all of our rushing around in our everyday life, all of our forcing in the face of the fear of these times, we often do not make the effort simply to find this state of deeper connection.

Also, if you chanted aloud, you may have realized that you were finding your own resident tone and pitch. You may have had it on the very first syllable, or it may have taken you considerable time to land on it. But as each of us finds our tone and pitch, the particular right vibration at this particular time, a sense of harmony and balance will descend over us. We will sense the appropriateness of our sound in this particular moment. This too is an experience of oneness.

Chant as long as you like. When you are finished, as always, locate and express your attitude of gratitude for this feeling of peace.

◆   ◆   ◆

7

Sparkling Prayers

In my personal vision, the Holy Spirit appears as a whirling cloud of beautiful mist filled with silver and gold specks. Within that mist, I see sparkling jewels. Rubies, diamonds and more, all vibrating at different frequencies. This cloud of mist, or perhaps I should say cloud of divine witnesses, reflects to me the unlimited and boundless nature of Holy Spirit. This is my own unique perception of the Holy Spirit, and I am describing it because there is no way to articulate the sacred energy of God except in a way that we can experience. God cannot be defined in terms. God needs to be experienced. Theology is not the study of God through books and brains. The original meaning of theology was the study of God through experience. As human beings, it is our need and desire to experience God. It is also our birthright.

That others have experienced this same perception affirms my own knowing. Turning again to the words of Hildegard of Bingen in her book *Scivias*:

> The Holy Spirit is a Burning Spirit. It kindles the hearts of humankind. Like tympanum and lyre it plays them, gathering volume in the temple of the soul. Holy Spirit is Life-

giving-life, all movement. Root of all being. Purifier of all
impurity. Absolver of all faults. Balm for all our wounds.
Radiant life, worthy of all praise, The Holy Spirit resurrects
and awakens everything that is.

This was Joseph Campbell's idea as well, when he said, "People say that what we're all seeking is a meaning for life. I think
that what we're really seeking is an experience of being alive, so
that our life experiences on the purely physical plane will have
resonance within our innermost being and reality, so that we
can actually feel the rapture of being alive."

Such a feeling of rapture certainly is awakened by our becoming personally aware of the enlightened individual Spirits under
the direction of the Holy Spirit. Through this rapture, we experience wholeness as we come to know the Holy Spirit as the
container for all of the Christed Spirits. These are the spirits
that can be of true service to you. One way to make the connection with these Spirits is, when you pray, announce your intention to communicate with those Spirits under the direction of
the Holy Spirit. That's what you will get. It's that simple. There
is no complex scholarly theology behind it. Once this experience of the Holy Spirit and the Holy Spirits resonates within
you, you also will experience its outward expression in your life
in some form or other. You may feel the rapture Joseph Campbell speaks of or you may get a sparkling vision like mine, but
somehow Holy Spirit and perhaps many of the individual spirits
will become known in your life.

The point of this discussion is that we need to make our
prayers sparkle every bit as brightly as our vision of Holy Spirit,
as brightly as the stars and moon in the night sky. If we can
experience the truth that this sparkle is the vibration of commu-

nication from God to us, then our human awareness takes on the intention to respond to God with just as bright a light. The need for this recognition is emphasized in the following words of the Moslem saint Hasan Basri, who lived one century after Prophet Mohammed. He is said to have related this parable:

> I saw a child coming toward me, holding a lighted torch in his hand. Where have you brought the light from? I asked. He immediately blew it out, and said to me, O, tell me where it is gone, and I will tell you from where I fetched it.

The appreciation of the sparkling of stars set against the black sky of night also was reflected in ancient Persian mystery schools that provided a monastic-type training for the soul. Lengthy ceremonies were conducted in the ancient *mehrab*, the word for prayer house in the Farsi language, a dome-shaped structure with a door that always faced east. Moon and stars were painted on the ceiling, creating an all-night atmosphere within the enclosure. The opening in the eastern wall permitted the rising sun to enter at dawn, bringing light that signaled an end to meditations and ceremonies. The intent was to create within the dome a replication of the cyclical day and night existence of earth, wherein the initiate could perceive divine possibilities rather than everyday limitations. From this process emerged the realization of one's life purpose, which the Persian mystics defined as service to the two divine attributes of joy, compassion and wisdom.

Embracing the sparkling nature of light, we come to realize that the sacred light that we are receiving comes from the same place that we want to reach with our prayers. Through the sparkle, God demonstrates his mode of communication to us. It's up to us to respond appropriately and effectively.

So how do we do this? Many ways certainly, but most obviously, with our voices, our words. Our words are powerful beyond our realization. Jesus addresses this clearly in Mark 11:22–25:

> Have the faith of God. I tell you the truth, if anyone says to this mountain, "Go, throw yourself into the sea," and does not doubt in his heart but believes that what he says will happen, it will be done for him. Therefore, I tell you, whatever you ask for in prayer, believe that you have received it, and it will be yours.

In Aramaic spirituality, the words of Jesus are breathed, chanted, intoned and prayed as a method for tapping into Christ consciousness. The words then lead to the movement of energy. In turn, experiencing the spark of the Holy Spirit becomes the main springboard for transformation and transcendence. Integrating this experience into a Christ-centered life becomes the individual's responsibility. The spark in me can ignite the spark in you, and the spark in you can ignite the spark in other people. This spark is the divine energy that is alive in all of us. When this spark ignites and consciousness is raised, you never have to feel alone again. You will never feel separated from God again. You will know it down deep in your being, and you will know that you know that you know. You have never been alone, you are not alone now, and you never will be alone. You are never separated from the Divine.

I encourage everyone to read the wonderful series of books by Masaru Emoto about the effects of words on water crystals. These books detail how water crystals have been photographed after being exposed to particular words, and the photographic images of the crystals are extraordinary. When positive, life-affirming words are pronounced over water, beautiful crystalline formations appear, resembling enlarged images of snowflakes that we all have seen. My favorite story in the first book, *The Hidden Messages of Water*, is about how the words of a Buddhist Monk affected an extremely polluted river over the course of a few months. The monk simply sat on the shore of the river and literally spoke the names of attributes of God such as love, peace, harmony and joy over the water. To the amazement of researchers, the polluted water became clear enough to drink. When we consider that at least 70 percent of our physical bodies are made up of water, this can inspire us to speak over our own body about its health issues. Further, if we consider how much of our planet is made up of water, why do we not simply speak to the planet for its healing. Dr. Emoto's work illustrates the extreme practicality of recognizing the effects of prayer and working to create those effects.

Photographers at some of my recent retreats and workshops have found sparkling images in their own photographs taken during our healing ceremonies. Although the photographers thought they were simply taking shots of third dimensional ceremonial activity, they found after development that the photographs displayed shining circles of various intensities of brightness hovering over, under and around the ceremony participants. This, of course, is a previously observed phenomenon, as similar lights have shown up in other photos of spiritually infused events and sites for many years. At the Golden City, it's a common occurrence. The effect of these photos of lights creates powerful impressions on us. When these photographs are enhanced by computer, they display amazing mandalas reflecting a great scope of colors. As in the water photos of Dr. Emoto, the sparkling of light appears in a dimension that cannot be perceived by our naked eyes. When such beautiful and unusual images appear to us, we are moved profoundly in the core of our beings. We take this as a blessing, an indication that the divine realm beyond our eyesight is sending us indications of deeply primordial structures of life, and those structures are beautiful.

It is always good to be amazed by such phenomena since that amazement raises our vibration about the nature of our existence and further inspires us to seek the continual company of God. But at the same time, we do not want to allow ourselves to be overwhelmed. These photographs demonstrate what can happen to the molecular makeup of the atmosphere when we pray. But as we call to mind the Sufi proverb, "Trust in Allah, but tie up your camel," we understand that this opportunity offers us the challenge to stay grounded as well. When we observe such beautiful phenomena, the temptation is to want to transport our minds and beings into that realm, possibly stay there, and perhaps even try to convince others that it is beneficial to dwell in that abstract level of reality while ignoring the three dimensional material world. We believe we have proof of God's existence in the light of our photographs, and we desire to live within that proof rather than in the rest of God's creation.

If this is our tendency, it is good to remember the old Zen story about the *roshi,* or Japanese Zen master, and his young meditation student. Zen, of course, is the Buddhist practice of sitting, breathing, and awaiting enlightenment. Lots of stuff comes and goes through the mind during this process. In this story, after sitting yogi-style and watching his breath moving for hours and even days, the student suddenly shouts, "Roshi,

Roshi, I have reached enlightenment! I see the great, beautiful, shining, golden Buddha sitting in complete peace! He is surrounded by jewels and is wearing a crown of glittering diamonds. It is a wonderful, wonderful vision! I am enlightened."

And the master replies, "That's all right, my child, just keep breathing. It will go away."

The point here is that we do not want to get obsessed with the other side, no matter how beautiful our visions and images of that dimension of Holy Spirit. After all, the third dimensional world is also a creation of God. Our purpose in visiting the deeper dimensions is not to prove that they exist but rather to perceive the transcendent divine qualities of those dimensions and bring them back and manifest them in our everyday reality. The sparkling images of our transcendent experiences inspire our minds with the knowledge of these qualities, such as unconditional love, truth, justice, and service. Then, as we continue breathing and the images dim, we find that our lives have been imbued with opportunities and means to ground those qualities into third dimensional existence and action. If we keep our focus, we can realize such work as our personal mission.

Taking on such a mission was one of the many accomplishments of Yogananda, who came from India to America early in the 20th century and established what is now a worldwide spiritual organization that has brought about much good. If you have read his classic book, *Autobiography of a Yogi,* you know that Yogananda was fully conversant with the realms of the Spirit. Yet there is a most revealing story about his understanding of the need to ground spiritual perception in reality.

When Yogananda was looking to establish an organizational center, some of his followers drove him up Mount Washington in Los Angeles, California, to show him a particular building.

Halfway up or so, they stopped before a large but rather simple log structure they thought would remind their teacher of an ashram of his native India. But Yogananda was not responsive to the site and asked to be driven further up the mountain. There they came upon an aging but once-grand hotel that Yogananda recognized instantly needed only some renovation to serve as his center. He wanted to manifest the best and highest possible appearance for God, not just something that was familiar and easy. If our work is for the glory of God, why wouldn't we want the best and highest that we can imagine or create?

Our focus now reveals itself as a process of two steps. First, making our prayers sparkle as brightly as God's images appear in our own visions. And second, grounding our perceptions of God's light into reality here on our planet. Our next question is, since words contain so much power, what are the best words?

Again, namasmarana-chanting the name of God-is a wonderful place to start. The sound of God emanates a creative energy. Call it an original blessing. It's the sound of an energy, a grace coming forth from this creative entity we know as God, the pure being. And that sound comes to us and also emits from us through the breath. All of the cosmos breathes life. That's why you find the early mystics always praying outdoors. They catch the energy from the trees, the flowers, plants. All is breathing, all is breath, all is the breath of the Divine. If we consciously practice breathing, this simplest of all living activities, we allow the energy of the Holy Spirit to enter into our bodies, move through our bodies and restore the wholeness of our beings.

Once that original sound of the name of God comes forth, the healing process is set in motion. To get a glimpse of what this entails in terms of the physical universe, we can turn to the description of our microscopic world as put forth by quantum mechanics, the branch of science that originated early in the 20th century. To explain a complex process in as brief and simple a way as possible, quantum physicists now tell us that when our attention is focused in a particular way, that focus in essence turns into a particle and assumes its position in the material world. Wave reality becomes particle reality. Creation starts to happen. That's what this is all about.

I've been very fortunate that at particular times in my life, individuals come and share their expertise on many subjects with me. That's part of what keeps my mission going. As I learned the principles of basic quantum theory, I realized this approach to understanding the universe makes sense when it is applied to particular passages in the ancient wisdom teachings. Before I knew it, quantum theory was making sense throughout my understanding of the Divine. I knew this approach could be utilized to understand how to bring healing to other people and also to myself through my experience of the Divine.

From this perspective, there were quantum physicists thousands of years ago telling the creation story. We understand anew the meaning of "God said let there be light," because light is what God is. God is pure being, pure essence. Only light can come forth from God. But we also know that light is energy, so Holy Spirit is this light energy that is always creating. That's why, even if you don't know it, you have a new body every few years. In a few weeks, your stomach lining cells completely change. In a few more weeks after that, those cells have left your body, replaced with others. If we can only awaken the true and whole self into its own place of constant renewal, the new cellular structures do not have to replicate old patterns that manifest disease. New health can enter us, literally through our breathing, as new organic material replaces the old. The wholeness of divine intent, otherwise known as wave reality, becomes particle reality. This is the inner process of spiritual healing.

Our prayers therefore want to be sparkling because the sparkle is the constant expression of divine energy that effects quantum change throughout our bodies and, indeed, throughout our entire web of existence. This is how healing moves from one physical location to another, light flashing and flashing as energy moves. In the simple and classic explanation of physicist H.P. Stapp, "An elementary particle is not an independently existing, unanalyzable entity. It is, in essence, a set of relationships that reach outward to other things."

This fluidity of outward reaching is also the principle of distant healing. Our intent travels as quickly as the lights flash. There's no distance here. If you actually sit down and try to project healing, that's really too much work. All you have to do is learn to make the connection to God. Who knows exactly how to project and where? You do not need to tell Holy Spirit where to go. There are many, many trillions of cells in our body, each one with its own little brain, its own nucleus that knows what every other cell in the body is doing. This structure is programmed for health. Certainly we can interfere with this health with our programming, belief patterns, spoken words and so forth, but the cells are created to know what to do if we stay out of the way by practicing continual devotion.

As we accept this reality of ourselves as extensions of divine light, everything begins to change. The writings of Saint Paul remind us, "You are children of the light." As we've discussed, when God said, "Let there be light," energy emanated from the divine consciousness, from God's own spirit and compassion and tenderness and love. This is the foundation of the material world, and every vibration that went out from the words "let there be" became a manifestation of the very energy of God.

There is a statement in the Letter of James, "All good comes from the Father of light." What's the light he's speaking of? It's us. We are the emanations of God's light. That why Jesus taught. "Don't hide your light under a bushel basket where the people cannot see it. Let your light shine forth." Mystically, this is truth. God is light energy and so are we, because we are emanations of God's own light. Our perception of this sacred laser of God diminishes any illusion of darkness.

Think for a moment of how far we've advanced in our current technology and medicine. We now value and utilize medical treatments that are evolving out of light and sound. Primordial light was the first element in the creation of the universe, but our understanding has drifted so far from that reality in recent centuries. Now we are beginning to bring that reality back and we can personify it in our lives as a sacred essence. We can give this reality of light any name we want. We can call it our teacher or master, such as Jesus or Yogananda or the name of some other individual from a different tradition who has gone to the other side. We can give it the various names that Native Americans give to God, Great Spirit, *Wakan Tanka,* and so on. Whatever name we give to God, we are doing so in order to personify the divine light in the way that is most meaningful to us on a personal level. In our prayers, our communion, our meditation and our contemplation, we can make it our purpose to see only light. As we enter into that light, we recognize that it is a laser beam that corrects and heals anything that is in need within us. When such healing happens, people refer to this process as a true healing miracle.

This is also the principle of creating peace in our world. As we acknowledge our loss of soldiers and civilians in war, of children in poverty and epidemics, of entire communities in natural disasters, we must create a literal force of light that sparkles through the despair and grief of millions of human beings every single day. This force must be maintained. You and I, as individuals and as a group, have the power to generate that force. It is the responsibility and possibility for each of us. This point is made strongly by Philo, the ancient Jewish philosopher who documented the Therapeutae. He penned this ancient truth that still holds firm today: "Households, cities, countries and nations have enjoyed great happiness when a single individual has taken heed of the good and the beautiful. Such people liberate not only themselves; they fill everyone they meet with a free mind." Is this not a beautiful and worthwhile goal for us all?

An examination of Tibetan Buddhism becomes relevant in terms of similar perceptions about this age of the spiritual evolution and direct communion with Holy Spirit. Ancient Buddhist scriptures reveal that two thousand five hundred years ago, the historical Buddha Shakyamuni proclaimed a future age when a being called "Medicine Buddha" would come to serve humankind. (We need to understand that the term "Buddha" merely means "the enlightened one," and there are many different Buddhas in this tradition.) Remember, the origins of the Therapeutae has been traced to the ancient monastic tradition of Indian Buddhists, and parallels between the Christian perception of Holy Spirit and Buddha's description of Medicine Buddha are obvious. Be aware once again that this story is most powerfully read from the perspective of an energy paradigm, a mystical teaching declaring that the force of Spirit is alive and real.

Buddhist scriptures tell us that when the historical Buddha first described Medicine Buddha to a gathering of followers in India, he left them with a shining image they could relate to and remember. Medicine Buddha was described as a being of lapis lazuli blue. Lapis lazuli is a shining stone, and the highest quality lapis is dotted with gold speckles of light against a deep blue like the stars shining against the darkness of night. Tibetan tradition claim the lapis is a stone that fell from outer space and thus provides a glimpse of the beauty that pervades the universe beyond our planet. This is the same shining beauty as my own perception of Holy Spirit.

The revelation about Medicine Buddha is said to have come while Shakyamuni was teaching to a large crowd of followers at a place called Vaishali in northern India, near the border with Nepal. A disciple named Manjushri asked the Buddha, "In the future when you are gone, when your teachings and general spiritual practices are in decline, when the human beings in this world are spiritually impoverished, who will save the people from their own attachment, anger and ignorance (the three 'poisons' of Buddhist teachings)?"

In response, the Buddha explained to the entire assembly about an ancient being of Lapis Lazuli color called the Medicine Buddha who would manifest in the future. By relying on Medicine Buddha and just by reciting his name, living beings could be cured of both mental and physical sickness. Shakyamuni also explained how to make a spiritual connection with Medicine Buddha through devotion and meditation. While Shakyamuni was giving this teaching, the disciple Manjushri realized through clairvoyance that many listeners were finding it difficult to believe in the existence of Medicine Buddha. So, prostrating himself in the Buddhist tradition, he made another request. "Lord Buddha, in order to remove doubts from the minds of all your followers, can you please demonstrate clearly that Medicine Buddha exists?"

The ancient writings report that the Buddha immediately absorbed himself into a deep concentration, and the people saw light rays emanating from his heart, inviting the Medicine Buddha to Vaishali. It is written that Medicine Buddha then manifested as a beautiful being of lapis lazuli blue before the people with his two main disciples, six other similar Medicine Buddhas and a large retinue of other disciples. The entire assembly could see Medicine Buddha and his group directly, and their doubts were dispelled on the spot. Buddha then gave instructions on how to recite the Medicine Buddha mantra for oneself and for others, such as the sick and dying, and how to perform many different healing rituals.

It is said that all those present witnessed the manifestation and rejoiced and developed a deep, unshakable faith in Medicine Buddha. Today, Medicine Buddha practice is the Tibetan tradition's most prominent method for spiritual healing.

Meditation

Buddha without Form

For many years, my public message has been that I have no intention of converting anyone to anything. My work is simply to offer a way of connecting to God. If you are a Christian, the goal is that you become a better Christian. If you are a Hindu, the goal is that you become a better Hindu. The Dalai Lama's message is identical as he considers the West's growing fascination with Tibetan Buddhism. "Learn from Buddhism if it is useful to you," he writes. "But do it as a good Christian or Jew or Muslim or whatever you are, and then be a good friend to us Buddhists."

The following meditation is a variation on the traditional Medicine Buddha mantra. Like all Buddhist teachings, this practice stresses the principle of the impermanence of all form. Unlike most Tibetan meditation practices that require formal empowerments by ordained lamas, the Medicine Buddha mantra is considered so essential in these times that lamas recommend its practice even without a formal empowerment ceremony. (If you are interested in personally experiencing these empowerments, they are conducted on occasion in the many Tibetan Buddhist centers around the world.) People in Western cultures now practice various versions of this meditation, learning from teachers and books and recordings. In doing so, they are following the Dalai Lama's advice: "Remember, you are a Westerner. If you want to practice an Eastern philosophy such as Tibetan Buddhism, you should take the essence and try to adapt it to your cultural background and conditions."

If you want to add an authentic feel to this ancient devotion, hold a *mala*, or prayer beads, as you chant this variation of the Medicine Buddha meditation. Tibetans traditionally hold the mala in their left hands and move one bead for each repetition of the mantra. An alternative is to move the beads with your fingers as you go along, not counting the mantras but just knowing that you are pulling more energy into yourself with each bead moved.

To begin, visualize the blue Buddha, sparkling, appearing before you. See the universally known image of the sitting Buddha. His color is lapis lazuli, a beautiful deep, dark blue, sparkling with gold flecks. Remember, though I'm using "he" as a reference point, a Buddha is a fully realized and whole being, so there is no need to attribute either male or female qualities to your vision. If you are inclined to research the Medicine Buddha, you will discover several unique aspects of appearance to add to your visualization, such as the way he holds his hands and the objects he holds. But for now, simply see the blue Buddha.

Breathe and relax as the full image of this beautiful blue Buddha comes before you.

There are two ancient vibrational languages, Aramaic and Sanskrit, meaning the sounds of these languages actually move energy within our beings. Here is an opportunity to chant the Medicine Buddha mantra in Sanskrit. When your Buddha is visualized fully, chant:

Tayatha Om Beckanze Beckanze
Maha Beckanze
Randza Samungathe Swaha

Phonetically, it sounds like this:
Tay-a-ta Om Bay-kan-ze Bay-kan-ze Ma-ha Bay-kan-ze
Ran-ze Sa-mun-ga-tay So-ha

In essence, the chant begins by addressing the universal energy (Tayatha); chanting the ancient sound of creation (Om); repeating the Medicine Buddha's name (Beckanze) three times, each time going into deeper healing; and closing by calling: Master of Liberation, This is Perfect Timing (Ranze Samungathe Soha). Here is a breakdown of the individual translated terms:

Tayatha: An opening call: Now Listen.

Om: The sound of creation, the primordial creative force.

Beckanze Beckanze: The Medicine Buddha's name in Sanskrit. To say this name is the same as decreeing: Healing, Healing. We are calling the Medicine Buddha to provide healing to our physical body and our mentality.

Maha Beckanze: Great Medicine Buddha. Deepest Healing. Calling for the release and surrender of all subtle imprints of our past experiences that might cause trouble or illness in the future.

Randza: Highest Lord, Master.

Samungate: On the holy path of liberation.

Swaha: Auspicious, perfect timing.

Repeat this chant a few times, moving prayer beads if you are using them. Tibetans usually repeat in cycles of seven during short sessions. Longer meditations may include 108 repetitions, one for each bead on a full-sized mala.

As you are sitting, breathing, visualizing and chanting, allow feelings of healing and peace to literally wash over you and through you. Feel the healing presence of the Buddha. Know that you know that your body is healing of whatever ailments you may have. See the blue body of the Buddha as whole and sparkling with pure health, and then take that full essence into your own body. The Buddha is fully and wholistically healthy, and you can be too.

Now move your focus away from yourself and look out onto the world around you. Know that if all people and all nations are willing for just a moment to feel the presence and vibration of this Creator force, for just that moment there is peace. Know that if this vibration can bring peace for one moment, the peace can stay for two moments. If for two, then for three. If peace can remain for three moments, it can sustain for one hundred billion moments. And then eternally. Feel the truth of this in the vibration of the Creator force running through your nervous system and the rest of your body as well.

Continue chanting until you sense it is time to stop. Now, focus again on the blue Medicine Buddha. Realize that you have taken in the divine qualities of peace and healing and that it is time to release your visualization. As you watch the Buddha's form slowly dissolve, realize the impermanence of even this beautiful vision. At the same time, acknowledge the ongoing nature of the sparkling energy that you have received. It is a powerful surrender to release this Buddha of energy to fade back into the vast formlessness of the universe.

Notice now that, even after Medicine Buddha has vanished from your visualization, you still feel the sparkling of the energy throughout your nervous system, healing every disease, every infirmity, every injury, on every level. Feel the healing Buddha with you completely, and with everyone else on earth. Feel the Buddha's powerful desire and determination for peace throughout the planet. Breathe deeply one final time and know that Medicine Buddha's lapis lazuli sparkling power of healing and peace are filling the universe around you.

Now, realize that the Medicine Buddha has dissolved ...

and the Buddha has no form.

◆   ◆   ◆

8

The Need for Discernment

As we progressively open ourselves to receive and reflect the light, the flow from the Divine makes itself known to us in ways that are ever more obvious to our physical senses. Synchronicities may appear increasingly in our day-to-day existence and take on significant meanings. Our dreams may become vivid and revealing. We may develop the clairvoyance to see wondrous images or the clairaudience to perceive sacred whisperings. Receptivity to the words of an inner voice often is among the first of these gifts of the Holy Spirit.

But these modes of connection to our primordial source do not come to us without their own unique challenge. To put it most directly, that challenge is to "know thyself." When it comes to dealing with human perception, discernment can be a tricky business, and there comes the time that each of us must perform a reality check on what we are doing. That's why every authentic spiritual tradition offers its own version of how to know when you're listening to God rather than to words being transmitted from less authoritative sources. There are many ways to double-check the authenticity of what we perceive, but our spiritual community often is the most powerful and important element of verifying our discernment. I have my own community of spiritually aware people around me, and I use them quite often as a sounding board for the guidance that I personally receive. It was most interesting and revealing to me, during the India visit, that Sri Bhagavan also revealed that he demands that his own guidance be confirmed by two of his most trusted disciples before he accepts and acts on that guidance.

Why is such demanding discernment necessary? Because we all want so sincerely to know God, to hear the Divine voice of wisdom and counsel and guidance. We know this connection to the higher realm is a very good thing, and we want to find a way to make it happen. In today's world, there are many spiritual books to read, many teachers with whom to study, many churches and other pathways offering to fulfill this desire to connect. But no matter which path or teacher or technique we choose, every seeker of God must develop this sacred skill of discerning the true presence and intent of Divinity. When God speaks to us, we need to know how to listen. We humans may make lots of mistakes and goof up a lot of opportunities during our lives, but we don't want misunderstanding God's intent to be one of those goof-ups. Through the silence we can connect with the still, small, sacred voice within that loves us and can guide and direct us effectively. But it is essential to develop discernment as to whether what we are hearing is from God or from some aspect of our ego.

For one thing, we must ground ourselves with the understanding that the part of our beings that listens appropriately to God is that which we call the true self. This is the witness of all we see and hear. The true self is detached from our personal thoughts and feelings. It has no personal agenda other than objectivity. It participates in no expectations, no comparisons, no judgments. The true self does not want to further our careers, our love lives or our reputations.

Realizing the true self, the purpose of mystics for millennia, arises through the development of a particular condition within each person. This condition is what we call emptiness or silence, and each tradition identifies this rarified essence in its own way. Ancient Greek writings refer to this inner state of being as *kyros* time, when our everyday ideas of time and space cease. In Tibetan Buddhism, it is called *rigpa,* the wisdom state of pure light. Praying in order to release our third dimensional considerations and meditating to hallow out a space within ourselves are steps in creating this silence. The more proficient we become in entering this state, the richer our meditative experiences. Ultimately, this silence becomes our personal ground for accessing our capacities to know the world of Holy Spirit intimately, to heal and to generate peace.

Reaching silence is a significant step on our pathway to discernment, so we need to know how to identify this inner condition when it appears, which may often be during meditations but also at any other time as well. Our tendency is to think of silence as synonymous with absolute quiet, but that is not true. Silence is our primordial condition and that condition embraces all that we can experience, including sound. Remember, when we pray as Solomon prayed, we are inviting the fire of Holy Spirit into our personally hallowed out vessel, and that new vessel is our silence. As Holy Spirit enters, we perceive our vessel filled and vibrating with a dynamism unprecedented in our human experience. Suddenly, our silence emerges as pure potential to act for God. If we have been successful in releasing our ego concerns and our fears during our preparatory practice, we experience this dynamic potential with an extraordinary confidence. We recognize the divine nature of our experience and, just this easily, we know we are in contact with God. At this point, the appropriate focus for the individual becomes discernment of the true nature of that which is revealed by God within our vessel of silence and putting those revelations to work in everyday life.

This presence of the true self offers us the opportunity to see God from a new, broader, deeper perspective of ongoing spiritual discernment. Once awakened, this discernment presents a view of the world through an energetic paradigm, enabling us to understand more deeply the work of Holy Spirit within and around us. In fact, spiritual discernment can be seen as the primary function of the true self. Absorbed in the presence of the Holy Spirit, the self utilizes spiritual discernment to see God performing that which one is called to do. In other words, if our own personal purpose is simply "to be"; God will take care of everything else. The more consistently we hold this understanding as our central core of perceiving and understanding all existence, the more we welcome God to influence the world through our being.

Spiritual discernment is the alternative to reliance on doctrine or dogma to know God's will and to walk our own pathway. So the question comes, just what is this discernment? How does it arise? Beyond continuing our meditations and prayers, is there anything we can do to encourage its presence? The answer is yes.

One important thing is to turn your awareness to remembering what and who you really are. You are a human being, not a human doing. We came into this world as manifestations of the Divine Spirit called human beings. This means that our natural state of being is capable of manifesting our highest, most Godlike qualities. By simply being, we are living, creating, loving. We don't have to think about doing those things and we don't have to make an effort to do those things. If we can just be, the creative powers of God will manifest a beautiful existence all around us. We did not come into this world as human doings, as people obsessed with schedules, accomplishments and recognition. These obsessions came later on, when we forgot who we were as emanations of the Presence and began to value the opinions of other humans over our contact with God. Remembering who we are means slowing down, looking at ourselves and experiencing the joy of being. It means keeping a sense of humor about ourselves, not taking ourselves so seriously. This is incredibly important.

In a prominent place on my altar at home, I keep my framed print of a painting known as *The Laughing Jesus*. This is the most powerful visual representation of Jesus for me personally, because it always reminds me of how necessary it is for me to stay in touch with my own inherent humor and to use it in my own teaching. Years ago when I was studying to become a priest, I was very fortunate to be in a particular Benedictine abbey where many of the monks were mystically orientated. In other words, they experienced God. One of my favorite monks, who later became my spiritual adviser for three years, was Father Ignatius Hunt. He was one of the translators of the Dead Sea Scrolls. What I loved most about him were an absolute sensitivity, his joy, compassion and sense of humor. He stood about six-six and he spoke in a very deep voice like a professional radio announcer. I always was amazed to watch him teaching a group of children and speaking to them on their level of ultimate simplicity, and then walk down the hall and teach his class of M.A.

students, speaking on their level of sophistication. His transition was seamless. I knew he had something special.

One day in class he was demonstrating the Book of Acts when he was struck by the divine energy. He jumped up on his desk and he began to act as one of the Apostles, demonstrating how to heal the sick. This was back in 1965, a year before I was ordained, and no one was teaching this sort of thing. I thought, "Healing? What's he talking about?" Then he stopped and got very serious. He said, "Unless the Christian church returns to its mission of healing, it will collapse and die."

This powerful but unorthodox statement came through Father Ignatius' spiritual discernment and found its way into my consciousness through his humorous presentation. And they helped shape my life. Today, look at the truth in those words. The Christian church has not returned to its mission of healing that demonstrates the light energy of the Divine Spirit, which has always been alive and well. Today we see the church, like many other traditions, in a state of collapse, a state of ruin. However, I don't see this as a bad thing. I think it's exciting. It reminds me of the mythological bird called the Phoenix, which was engulfed and destroyed by its inner fire, only to rise again from its own ashes. This collapse of the modern church is like the fire of the divine breath of God that totally engulfed the phoenix before it rose as a new bright creation. That, to me, is what Christian, Hebrew, Hindu and other sacred literature is about. It's about our remembering that we are not this body and we are not physical beings first and foremost. We came from divine light into being, we are spiritual beings experiencing a physical existence and eventually we will return to sacred unity with God.

It was also Father Ignatius from whom I learned to read scriptures as stories of energy events. One of his first principles was, "You can never read sacred wisdom literature with human eyes. You must read all sacred wisdom literature with the eyes of the heart, with the eyes of the Spirit. Then, as you sit in the silence in this awareness, revelations come to you. Then comes the courage and the strength to listen to those revelations and be guided by them." So many of my own teachings and understandings about the path of Jesus have come this way. Then later, these concepts often are verified and explained through other people with whom I am brought into contact.

This approach to mystical understanding is consistent with the observations of the Dalai Lama. He has explained there are three levels on which spiritual writings can be taken: the literal, the symbolic and the mystical. Ultimately, much of Buddhist teaching is aimed at guiding students to reach the mystical level. "There is an enormous difference between a path created with the ordinary mind and a path created through wisdom," the Dalai Lama has pointed out. That wisdom path leads to the realization of rigpa, the innermost nature of mind. The attributes of rigpa are virtually the same that we attribute to the silence. "Rest in rigpa," he states, "and within that state, thoughts will simply vanish." In addition, one of Tibetan Buddhism's most prominent modes of spiritual transmission is known as the "ear whispered tradition," a clear reference in this ancient tradition to the clairaudient connection to the Divine.

The followers of Jesus and Buddha share a common interest in emphasizing discernment of the original nature and intention of these spiritual masters. Neither Buddha nor Jesus wrote down their teachings. In both instances, our earliest renderings of their words were written by others after their deaths. Further, today's versions of these writings, which became the canons of religions that sprang up around these two masters, were shaped by the governing religious establishments of their times. Today, if you wish to understand Buddha's original teaching, you must go through the same process as those who want to study the deepest reality of Jesus' teachings. For one thing, you can study the original Sanskrit and Aramaic and understand the context of their times. But as you hallow out a space and then allow Holy Spirit to fill that space, you also must develop discernment as to how you are going to express that Spirit in your earthly life. On this path, as the Dalai Lama often emphasizes, doctrine gives way to the inner opening of Spirit. "I am just a simple monk," he has proclaimed many times. "My religion is kindness."

So how does our development of silence and then discernment play out in our everyday spiritual practice? Once we begin receiving what we think are whispers or images from God, what are the practical steps we can take to confront our human limitations in such perceptions?

Let's say, a problem arises in your life. This problem may concern health or finances or relationships or your spiritual path. Or maybe all these. You decide to seek divine guidance on how to heal. You practice your personal discipline of opening to sacred directive. You may pray, breathe deeply or sit in lotus position. In time, your personal silence comes. Then, perhaps as chills run up your spine, there also comes that quiet inner voice. And the voice says, "You are to quit your job, stop taking your medicine and move your family to a spiritual community halfway around the world."

Now I ask you, are you sure that's God speaking?

During forty years of teaching the divine presence and creating environments in which people actually experience that presence, I have observed many people experience difficulty in telling the difference between the true voice of God or any sacred spirit who can guide us effectively and all those other voices that rumble around in our heads. Or in a word, difficulty in practicing discernment. I cannot count the times people have shared with me their experiences of following guidance about major life changes, only to discover through bitter experience that the changes didn't work. Then they blame God. The truth is, the problem lies a lot closer to home. Just because we recite the words of a prayer or cross our legs in lotus position doesn't mean the next words we hear necessarily come from God.

Don't get me wrong. Seeking guidance through prayer and meditation is what I teach and what I practice. I myself pray and breathe and sit quietly to make that direct, vita connection to unconditional love and joy, and to God. But we all need to comprehend the deeper essence of our guidance, not just react to the surface words. Sooner or later, almost every seeker accesses direction from an inner voice about significant life matters, and we need to know how to listen. What we may not realize is that there are ways of examining the messages that come through. After all, people probably have been listening for God from the beginning of time. By now, we should have learned something.

What I have learned over my own years is that discernment challenges our self-understanding at a deep level. On the one hand, we need to develop a clear perception of the terms "ego" and "mind." On the other hand, we must experience God directly so that we recognize in our hearts the true feeling of divine consciousness. Otherwise, it is just too easy to glaze over the possibility that our ego, that mass of self-concern that wants to dominate our lives, may be strongly influencing the message we're receiving. Further, we tend to discount that the source of our messages could be the thoughts of humanity over the centuries-that collection of musings that we call the mind. If we're tempted to stop taking our medicine or move halfway around the world based on an inner directive, it really is a good idea to investigate the best ways to listen deeply.

Two basic cornerstones in discerning authenticity are, first, to apply our own wisdom to its limits and, second, as mentioned above, to consult our spiritual community. Consulting community for discernment is a practice common to all authentic wisdom traditions. Later in this chapter, I will share a few questions that a spiritual community can put forward to help determine the validity of guidance. But first, we can develop some common ground for understanding the influences that may surface during listening.

If you do not belong to a spiritual community, you can at least consult someone who has more experience in such matters than we ourselves. But I also want to point out that if you are not part of such a community, you might want to ask yourself, why not? What is stopping you from joining others in seeking a more wholistic understanding of the Holy Spirit? You may find out some interesting things about yourself as you pursue this answer.

Freeing ourselves from the clutches of ego in order to experience reality involves the same discernment as knowing the difference between God's voice and inner babbling. There is a directive that I love and admire for its simplicity and clarity. It is taken from the work of The Mother, the spiritual partner of Sri Aurobindo. She wrote, "To begin with ... know by experience the difference between mind and consciousness, two quite different things."

By "consciousness," The Mother is referring to the divine essence of authentic wisdom, that which we've been calling the true voice of Divinity. But her words also emphasize the distinction about "mind" common to Eastern thought that we have mentioned earlier. In the West, we tend to think that each person possesses an individual mind. In Eastern teachings, there is one mind of human consciousness, and all humans tune into that mind through individual intellectual processes. This mind, according to the Vedic teachings, comprises the thoughts of humanity over the entirety of our existence as a species. Individual humans, the teachings say, pick up impressions from mind in the form of thoughts, which then bring up feelings.

This mind web of connective thought enables us to perceive what one another is talking about, and thus provides stability in day-to-day life. But problems can emerge when we link our personal identities to the mind. Here in the West, everything from basic communication to our abstract ideas about God are observed and defined in terms of the mind. We find ourselves relying on the mind to register expectations, comparisons and judgments about the people and events that make up daily existence. Then we begin defining who we are in terms of these same expectations, comparisons and judgments. After we've built up the mind to a point of dominance in our lives, there is little room for other input such as intuition to register. We come to accept mind itself as being so powerful that we commence to consider it as the source of all being. We see it as the ultimate reality, rather than just a collection of thoughts.

So, when we sit down to meditate, the mind is the first source of information we're likely to encounter. All the collective thoughts of humanity's history are just out there waiting for us to pull them in, and our mental processes and individual histories serve as magnets to attract thoughts that relate to our egoic perceptions of ourselves, for better or for worse. If we are not prepared to discern what comes from mind and what comes from God, we can receive a very clear reading from mind and think it is from God.

This means that, if in that vast expanse of the thoughts of eons there exists a suggestion to move my family to an ashram a thousand miles away, I can pick up that suggestion. Further, if in the past I ever entertained the thought of such a move, that thought form in itself is enough to attract guidance to my listening.

Meditation masters learn to recognize mind input and allow it merely to evaporate. But unless we have trained for years like these masters, evaporation may not come easily. As a result, excessive self-concern, self-centeredness and self-pity, all conditions indicating the dominance of ego in our lives, may attract mind babbling that is confused with guidance from a deeper source. Because we believe so strongly in the mind, something special is necessary to restore our inner focus. That something special is the spiritual art of discernment that each of us is responsible for developing. In this sense, discernment is the key to the door of sacred knowledge. But how do we turn the key to unlock this door?

Let's return to The Mother's words, "… know by experience the difference between mind and consciousness, two quite different things." We have explored the meanings of mind and consciousness, but the true key lies in the phrase "know by experience." To gain this experience, we must test our concept, perhaps many times, in order to know, really know, what we're doing. Sometimes trial and error works. But a better testing takes the form of consulting our spiritual community.

Following is a set of suggested questions and considerations that a community might raise to clarify listening and validate personal guidance. These considerations are designed to cut through egoic concerns and influences in listening, and to help us recognize authentic guidance.

I also want to emphasize that these questions apply not only to information that you take in for yourself, but also to "readings" done for you by people who claim to be "channeling" information from sources on the other side. There are many, many sources out there that will tell you many, many things. You don't want to give away your personal power of choice to just anyone listening to words from some invisible source. Be smart. That said, here are some steps of guidance:

- Begin your process by acknowledging that one way God teaches is step-by-step and quite deliberate, and often our first understanding can be far distant from the ultimately intended sacred meaning. Even if a message comes from a sacred source, we need to test it effectively to be sure it hasn't been tainted by ego concerns. If I have a medical condition and I hear personal guidance saying to stop taking my medicine, is the proper reaction simply to halt all medications? Or is it to look into another treatment that could be more effective? Even if there is no egoic influence at work, we need to respond intelligently.

- Is the voice telling you something that you really want to hear, such as "you're going to make a lot of money doing this?" Is it praising you or declaring that you are "the chosen one?" Are you being stroked? Does this guidance inflate your image of yourself in any way, shape or form? If the answer to any of these questions is yes, watch out.

- Have confirmations for the guidance appeared in your personal universe? Confirmations might include hints such as an unexpected opportunity, a chance meeting with just the right person, or a relevant passage from sacred literature that just happens to flow into your thoughts, perhaps time and again.

- But as you stay aware for confirmations, are you uncritically interpreting ambiguous wording in spiritual guidance in the most favorable light for yourself? Are you searching too hard for omens in the atmosphere to confirm your listening? Is there a hidden agenda in your wanting certain words to mean certain things?

- Is the guidance building relationships and creating a more harmonious environment among people around you? Or is it creating disharmony and division? If you act on the advice from your listening, would you be invading or violating another person's space or rights? This can be one of the most obvious indicators. God creates harmony, not disharmony. If there is a struggle and the door is closing, it may be time to stop and go back within to listen for the true opening that will allow the Presence to reveal to us that which is hidden.

- Would this guidance, if followed, produce a healing effect on either you or someone else? If you were to follow this guidance, can you foresee an outcome that would release a burden from you? Even accepting that God does not create disharmony, could the guidance be designed to reveal something about your that you prefer not to face? Has truth about a personal weakness surfaced in such a way that you can release that weakness and step forward in your life? This would be a purpose of God.

- Does the guidance instill fear or does it strengthen your confidence and courage? Is the guidance bringing out a true talent that you haven't used fully? The voice of God does not set us up for ambush or failure. It sets us up for success.

- Even linguistics can give clues. For instance, is the wording original or a copy? Information from mind tends to be robotic, and it often puts forth word plays rather than clear, authentic, creative phrases. If you have been given a name for a project or a building, is it an authentically creative name or is it a word play on an existing name? God's vocabulary is quite extensive.

- If you sit down and meditate on your listening, can you go deeper and deeper into your perception of the spiritual direction existing beneath its surface meaning? God's voice rings true on many levels. As you go deeper, are the revelations consistent with the universal principles of unconditional love and joy?

While these questions can open the way for deeper understanding, no such list ever can be complete in terms of understanding guidance because there are too many variables. Still, this is a good place too start. Taking guidance to community for discernment can assure that both you and anyone else involved will be held accountable on matters large and small.

But at the end of the day, both literally and figuratively, there still remains nothing better than once again seeking contact with our deepest divinity. Back into meditation one more time. Sit quietly. Breathe deeply. Pray whatever prayer you love. The more deeply we are aware of ego and mind, the more profound the level of healing we attract. Listening with discernment, we know our guidance reflects sacred intelligence and unconditional love.

With this foundation, we can appreciate sacred writings such as this Biblical passage from 1st Corinthians 13:1–4:

> If I speak in the tongues of men and of angels, but have not love, I am only a resounding gong or a clanging cymbal. If I have the gift of prophecy and can fathom all mysteries and all knowledge, and if I have a faith that can move mountains, but have not love, I am nothing. If I give all I possess to the poor and surrender my body to the flames, but have not love, I gain nothing. Love is patient, love is kind. It does not envy, it does not boast, it is not proud.

And doesn't that say it all? Even as we discern deeply, we still must know that love is the answer to all. Blessed with this knowledge, we can establish a clear and powerful access to the voice of God, a voice always there in every moment. We simply need to know how to listen. And listening well is a big, big part of living in the light.

Meditation

Surrendering into Discernment

This is an expansion of a meditation that I have given people for many years. It centers around the chant:

I am God breathed.

In this exercise, you breathe in and then out, first deeply, then normally. On the in-breath, you chant aloud or silently, "I am." On the out breath, "God breathed." As you continue to inhale and exhale, you are experiencing the words, "I am God breathed." This is a wonderful centering meditation that can be practiced anywhere, anytime.

Now, we're going to take it a little deeper.

Assume your sitting position for meditation. Again, this can be in your most comfortable chair or in yoga lotus position or anything in-between. Whatever works for you. Breathe deeply.

As above, as you inhale and exhale, chant silently or aloud, "I am God breathed." Do as many repetitions as needed to enter into a deep state of relaxation. Close your eyes either fully or halfway into an unfocused gaze.

When you reach that deep relaxation, stop your chanting and sit still. Feel and experience the silence. Become even more aware of your breath moving in and out, in and out. Know that the vibration of God is traveling on that breath.

Fully aware of being in the Presence of God, we will go even deeper.

Now, from Chapter Three, we will chant again our Sanskrit mantra, "Om Sat Chit Ananda Om," meaning Being Consciousness Bliss. Either silently or aloud, "Om Saaachitaaanda Om." Continue for a few minutes, not until you are tired, but rather until you are elated.

Feel the feeling of this silent, powerful place of elation in yourself where this mantra reverberates. See this place, taste it, take in its fragrance, and hear its clear, resonant music. This is the place of the Holy Spirit, the place within you created by God.

Get to know this place of elation intimately, no matter how many return trips it takes. Repeatedly find this place in your meditations until you recognize and yearn for its comfort and joy. When you can locate this place effortlessly and thoroughly, you are practicing your capacity for discernment. In time, you will see that the same effort necessary to find this elation is also the effort necessary to discern the essence of God from the essence of the ordinary in all pursuits and thoughts. Whatever happens for you in this place of elation will be profound and rewarding. You can exit at any time simply by reciting an appropriate benediction such as, "Peace and harmony to all beings."

Each time you visit, stay as long as you wish, perhaps a bit longer with each visit. There may be times you won't want to leave and there is eternally more to experience here. You will know you are really accomplished when your daily existence actually converts itself into this place of elation. It's worth working for.

◆   ◆   ◆

9

After Enlightenment Comes Compassion

After the experience of enlightenment comes the practice of fusion with God. After hallowing out a space, we experience the light in whatever form it comes, whether through the bestowal of Diksha or through meditation or through realization brought on by reading and reflection. As that light inspires our personal devotion and enflames our prayers, we eventually become proficient in discerning the true nature of our relationship and communication with God. Then comes the time to turn our faces toward the ever-present but ever-elusive possibility of merging with the Divine.

Ramalinga, the nineteenth century Indian master serves as a spirit guide for the Golden City, emphasized to his followers that *mukthi,* or enlightenment, is not the final step on the spiritual path. He taught that there is a further and deeper progression, an actual merging with what he called the Grace Light, a fusion of humanity and the Divine. For Ramalinga, the study of this merging took the form of lifelong devotion. His flowing prose poetry speaks at length about the nature of the light, which he considered our primordial source, and of its essence and effects upon our physical body and psyche. He constantly expressed his yearning to merge with the light in ecstatic lyrics such as the following, taken from his collected works known in the Tamil language as *Tiru Arut Paa,* which translates into the English title, *Holy Poems Sweeter than Nectar:*

Oh, Lord of Eternal Love!
Only bestow on me the Golden Body,
You have melted with my heart.
Being fused with me, oh Supreme Love,
You have transformed my body with the Grace light

While many of his Indian devotees today focus on Ramalinga's teachings of devotional meditation to merge with the light, it is most significant that he always emphasized that devotion traveled with a companion of even greater spiritual significance. That companion is the practice of compassion toward all beings. In other words, the relationships we carry on with our fellow human beings is the most basic and essential way to spread the light of God throughout the human family. Thus, another of his most famous verses: "My Life and my Compassion are a single thing, not two; if Compassion would abandon my Heart, also my Life would abandon me".

Translating the feeling of compassion for all beings into action, we come up with the simple, direct, powerful concept of service to humanity. Service in this context is a way of being. Service is giving oneself over to feeling fully the need of humanity and then allowing God to direct us how, when and where to act. Service is the life essence that has driven the saints of all traditions. When Mother Theresa looked out on the streets of Calcutta each day, she did not see the overwhelming and seemingly insoluble problems that so many of us would see. Rather, she saw endless opportunities to serve. In such work, Mother Theresa found fusion with the Divine.

Up to this point, we have been discussing how to prepare and open ourselves to the glow of divine light and how to invite this sacred visitor into the core of our being. Now we are examining how to learn to live with and express this sacred visitor. In the Celebrating Life Ministries spiritual community that has grown around my work of the past fifteen years, service stands as the core of who we are. We can define this as service to God, service to others, service to community or even service to ourselves, so long as we remember that we truly don't want to be serving our egoic nature. Service is compassion in action.

There's an ancient Chinese proverb that says: "Before enlightenment, chop wood and carry water. After enlightenment, chop wood and carry water." The meaning is, of course, that enlightenment is just a passing experience. In Sri Bhagavan's terminology, a neuro-biological process of relaxing part of the brain while activating another part. This proverb teaches that after that process of light, life then goes on the same as before. But I prefer to expand this teaching by saying: "Before enlightenment, chop wood and carry water. After enlightenment, chop wood and carry water, but do it more efficiently than before and do it in the spirit of service."

If the experience of enlightenment is to become fully meaningful to us, it needs to show up in our daily activities. If we truly are in union with God, people will look at us and be unable to tell where we end and God begins.

This teaching on the nature of service has emerged in recent seasons as one ingredient in Celebrating Life's ongoing work with the Oneness Movement. Even after people travel to India and are trained in the diksha blessing, there remains the need to stay daily in tune with our own compassion for all beings and our service to those beings. When in tune in this manner, we begin to live full-time in a hallowed-out modality, in complete congruency with the Presence in each instant. Discernment becomes much easier, and we enter that condition that I call, "Knowing that you know that you know." It's inner knowledge with a focus and a purpose. The mind is quiet and we serve and it feels great. Planting the seeds of light through diksha and other methods is very important, but we cannot ever forget that the ultimate fruit of the seeds is consistently ongoing God realization. It's an ancient truth, and it's still valid today.

On the path of coming to know that we know that we know, we also come to realize that the ancient teachings have not been lost to today's seekers of truth. That's just a fabrication of people who haven't gone deep enough into themselves to refocus on the ancient wisdom. Beyond buried parchments in the desert and razed mystery schools of yore, the wisdom of God is all here and now, tying together past and present. We simply need to perceive it. It's not that God gave some teachings thousands of years ago, then some different ones hundreds of years ago, and some more the day before yesterday. The truth is the truth is the truth. But because our planet now has developed sophisticated means of war that include the possibility of self-annihilation, we need the full impact of this truth to emerge at a more immediate rate and with a greater intensity than ever before. We need compassion, we need the full sense of service and we need the power of Ramalinga's grace light.

From the Middle East to Central Asia, Europe, Africa and the Far East, teachings of the sacred wisdom were kept alive for centuries through mystery schools and monasteries. Elsewhere in the world, indigenous cultures handed down their own unique practices and oral traditions pointing to this same wisdom of compassion toward other beings. Through all these diverse cultures, the teachings dealing with the nature of the universe and all its inhabitants have been preserved. These teachings explain life in terms of the many forms of energy and the relationship between the conduct of humanity and these energy forms. We humans, if we can understand what the teachings are trying to tell us, have at our fingertips a way of living peacefully in harmony with nature and with one another. Further, the teachings reveal an approach to healing and peace that becomes a universal pathway when practiced one person at a time.

Through this understanding, world peace is a condition to be achieved on a foundation of authentic human compassion and being, not through edicts handed down from national leaders or through governmental agencies. Like spirituality, peace cannot be constructed effectively on doctrine or dogma. History shows us the power of people such as Gandhi, whose spiritual integrity altered the lives of millions of Indians. By fasting for his belief in justice through nonviolence, he stopped fighting among factions divided desperately along religious lines. Gandhi's actions were powerful because he was a man filled with God, filled with compassion, dedicated to serving the people. His ongoing devotional practice was Namasmarana, chanting the names of God. His personal chant was simply a repetition of *Rama, Rama, Rama*-God, God, God. To inspire those who followed him in the name of freedom, he prescribed simplicity. He wore a loincloth and sandals. He wove cotton thread and advised people to make their own clothing, and these practices became economic as well as spiritual means of growth in India. Because of his absolute commitment to devotion, compassion and simplicity, the integrity of the man became known to the world and the course of history changed. This is the power of authentic compassion and service. This is a dramatic manifestation of the authenticity of divine light in everyday life.

The central foundation of authenticity is that every human person is capable of developing into a being far beyond that which everyday society accepts as usual or normal. Most of us, however, must go through a dramatic transformation in order to pursue this pathway, and we usually perceive this as a change in how we think. As the Indian saint Shirdi Sai Baba observed a hundred years ago, "Mind is tricky, for it ensnares us in temptation. Restrain it to attain peace." Shirdi Sai Baba served all who came to him. Like Gandhi and like virtually all the fabled gurus of India over the centuries, Shirdi Sai Baba lived simply and with deep devotion. He spent most of his life in the southern Indian town of Shirdi and always wore a simple tunic and turban. He advised people to chant the names of God. Miracles of healing and other high spiritual accomplishments were credited to him. Today, almost a century after his passing, temples and centers devoted to Shirdi Sai Baba are still springing up all over the world. But the amazing thing is this is not a unified effort at all. Individuals in distant lands simply hear about or come into contact with the spirit of this amazing being and they are moved to connect with him on a deep level. Such was the power of Shirdi's own compassion that his light still is sparkling throughout the world.

Whether we are talking about Shirdi or Gandhi or Jesus or any other great master, in-depth study of their words and practices will reveal that they are talking about one particular way of being. A way of quiet inner essence, the simplicity that comes to a person through a process of growth and change. In ancient China, this same understanding was articulated by the sage Lao Tzu in the classic text *Tao Te Ching* more than two thousand five hundred years ago. In English, Tao is translated simply as "the way." But understand that this refers to a way of releasing, not a way of activity. In the words of Lao Tzu: "The practice of Tao consists of subtracting day by day; subtracting and yet again subtracting until one has reached inactivity."

The subtracting is the removing of egoic concerns. The inactivity is the silence of the Holy Spirit. The Presence itself.

The *Upanishads* comprise the ancient wisdom literature of India, the earliest composed centuries before the Buddha. While the Sanskrit meaning of *Upanishad* is accepted as "inner mystical teaching," the literal root meaning is "to destroy." This meaning refers to the ultimate spiritual knowledge of the self that destroys ignorance and inspires the individual to enlightenment. But the Upanishads also stress that there exists an elemental spiritual core within humanity that cannot be realized except through a particular lifestyle. This lifestyle embraces such practices as meditation and yoga, leading to self-realization and freedom from karma. In the writing of the Indian sage *Shankara* some 1,200 years ago, we find this summary of the wisdom of the Upanishads:

> The nature of the one Reality must be known by one's own clear spiritual perception; it cannot be known through a teacher. Similarly the form of the moon can only be known through one's own eyes. How can it be known through others? Who but the Atman (the absolute or eternal One being) is capable of removing the bonds of ignorance, passion and self-interested action?

As our study continues, we grasp that this sacred wisdom of merging with God through compassion is all one teaching, no matter its cultural inflection. Furthermore, it's the same teaching that's been coming down since time immemorial. It's the teaching that all spiritual seekers seek. Just to be sure we get it, let us ask again: what is this immortal secret of the mind and heart that sages teach and everyone else yearns to learn?

Simply put, the secret is that each of us can tune into the mind of God, unknowable though it may be to our own rationality, if we can just release all else that fills our consciousness and diverts our attention. The deeper and more effective our release of egoic concerns and negative thoughts, the deeper our hallowing out a sacred place within ourselves for Holy Spirit to enter. The more consistently and effectively we step away from the world's magnets of distraction, the fewer obstructions appear as blockages to Holy Spirit's acting through us. As Holy Spirit acts through us in the form of service, we find we are living, perhaps suddenly transformed, in a world of compassion. As we release our excessive concern with ourselves, compassion can fill us.

Of course, this is not a secret at all. It's what all the teachers have been teaching forever. So why don't we all just do it, just release ourselves from our past and our hang-ups and whatever? We don't do it because we can't hear the teachers properly. We listen with only our mentalities and so we don't perceive their full meaning with our spiritual discernment. Our minds tempt us to try to think it out, find a methodology, and develop a precise way of performing this releasing. Mentality is our tool of understanding existence, and therefore it wants to spell out everything in what amounts to a believable doctrine. But the so-called secret is that the divine experience is beyond mentality;

the mind alone can't get it. Still, the desire for methodology and technique remains the mental temptation, and that's why Shirdi Sai Baba advises us to restrain the mind.

In truth, it's not difficult to comprehend the words the teachers are teaching. It's clear that one must release whatever conditions are hindering one's personal evolution in order to hallow out a space. If we can release, Holy Spirit always is ready to step right in as a powerful guiding force. As Holy Spirit steps in, the true self emerges and the ego falls aside. The individual stops being obsessed with me, myself and I. This is the transformation we've come to know as self-realization. This is the big change we all want, even after the experience of enlightenment. But even as we accept and understand all this with the mind, the perplexing questions still echo in our inner ears: If it's this simple, how do I do it? Why can't I do it right now? What do the teachers actually mean by release? What was Solomon praying for when he prayed, "Release, release, release, release"?

For one thing, we must realize that release is far different from relief. Release is a permanent freeing of our being, not just a temporary distraction from whatever mental or physical pain we want to escape from. When we release our personal blockages, this is not just for the duration of the prayer or meditation we are practicing. We are releasing ourselves into a totally new and different lifestyle. We are becoming quiet inside. This means seeing God in all things by moving beyond the perception of duality. Release means letting go of the idea that evil exists as an alternative to good. We stop thinking in the black and white terms of evil and good. Rather, we must learn to recognize that life is filled with good, more good or less good. God, more God or less God. This is the same concept as seeing God in all things, praying without ceasing and always being in the presence of the Divine. This is far beyond the power of positive thinking. It's the experience of positive being.

If you decide to live in this state of positive being, however, you may have to make some big changes in your life. I certainly did. After completing my studies in the seminary, I did not want to accept the dogma and doctrine that had been passed down to me. I made a commitment to study and meditate on the sacred writings and see what revelations would come. A few years later when I actually began receiving revelations about the true nature of the teachings, I thought, "Oh my God." Remember, I was a Roman Catholic priest and therefore I was expected to perform and perpetuate that belief system. As the revelations continued, I also was prompted continually, year after year, to stand up on a podium and declare this truth so that peoples' lives could be changed. That's what Jesus did, and that's why the religious leaders of his time got ticked at him. He was wrestling control away from the leaders in order to free the people. Just as in those times, you and I are born desiring freedom, not bondage. Illness can bind us. Relationships can bind us. Religious beliefs can bind us. Jesus was teaching freedom, not dogmatic bondage. Freedom means trust in God's unlimited love for all people.

Although at first I honestly didn't know what to do, I eventually began to act on these revelations and teach and preach in a different manner. Many of my services began to center on healing practices. Over time, releasing my original limiting beliefs and replacing them with the evidence of positive experiences became extremely powerful in all aspects of my being. This has made all of the difference in my life and has opened me to allowing the grace of healing energy to pass through me and reach out to touch others. Discovering the discrepancies between the original teachings of Jesus and the formal doctrines of the church has never harmed my faith and trust in God. Instead, my faith and trust have been enhanced. In essence, realizing the truth of the nature of Jesus' teachings led directly to my life's work. It brought me home, in the truest sense of home. Years ago I wrote this praise poem about finding just the right place at just the right time in the world.

> I was home …
> home is that state of being
> where one discovers himself—
> discovers peace of mind
> discovers life in its fullest dimension
> discovers joy that is overflowing
> discovers true health and healing
> It is resting in God's arms
> a state of surrender
> Being home is what we all want
> Being free is what we all desire

This was my way of finding and knowing my own mission. To make your own process of releasing limiting beliefs work, it's up to you to examine what you believe is true. If your life is being directed by a belief that is not true for you, you must either discard that belief or make it true for you. Either way, you're moving in a positive direction. This is a move toward reclaiming your true spiritual essence, that wiring for God that was yours as you entered this life. But you have to be discerning in this process, especially about the effects of other people's influence on what is true for you. There is a statement in Isaiah to the effect that, "You are confused because you are seeking multiple counselors for advice." That's the human dilemma. If I don't get the answer I want with the first counselor, I keep going to another and another until I hear what I want to hear. One may be speaking for God and others might be just speaking off the tops of their heads, and we miss out by not listening and discerning the spiritual connection of the person from whom we are taking counsel. You personally must come to know what is right for you.

Many people who have come to the Celebrating Life spiritual family have come looking for their work in the world as well. The same is true for many who return from the enlightenment experience with Sri Bhagavan in India. My guidance to these people is always consistent. I say, to determine your purpose in life, be compassionate toward yourself. Look at your attributes. What is it you love to do? Are you doing what you love to do right now? If not, why not? Usually the first answer is, "I couldn't make a living doing that." How do you know? Have you tried it? In all probability, that may be among your most limiting beliefs and a good one to release. If you find the true mission intended for you by God, a mission involving work through which you can lift up humanity and find satisfaction in life, you will make a good living at it. That's the sort of thing that can come to you on a personal level, once you start releasing those things that limit you and hold you back.

Release is also another word for forgiveness. But there is a problem in the way most of us understand forgiveness. In Deuteronomy, God says to the people, "I lay before you life and death, blessing and curse. I bid you choose life, but the choice is yours." Let us look at the word forgiveness as meaning "giving forth." Instead of forgive, give forth. Give forth what? Blessings instead of curses. Another way to look at forgiveness is to understand that you are not condoning the poor behavior of another human being towards you. Rather, you are releasing all negative feelings from your own being about any aspect of that behavior. This is an aspect of forgiveness we really need to learn. I deal with people who say, "She hurt me thirty-seven and a half years ago," or "He hurt me forty-six years ago." Don't you think it's time to let it go? Unforgiveness creates our biggest energy leaks. If you feel depression, despair, hopelessness, look at the areas of your life where you are being unforgiving. It's time to release your intensity over these problems through forgiving.

As you travel along this compassionate road of positive being and forgiveness, you come to realize that it's good to make a conscious commitment to lay the ego aside as best you can. We simply have difficulty keeping concern with ourselves on the proper step on the staircase of life. We put it on the very top step, and that creates trouble. Given too much importance and focus, ego drives us into wanting control over our life experiences and wanting approval from other people. We then learn to operate either by overpowering others in whatever way necessary or through the silent plea, "Approve me, please. I'll do whatever it takes to get you to approve me."

Through letting go of the need for control and approval, the ego can be relocated to a lower step on the staircase of life. As the true self then arises, our destiny is placed under spirit direction for guidance. Then the ego, redirected into its proper position, becomes another agent of God to heal and restore us. Instead of obsessing on "I, me, my needs and my wants," the ego focus changes to how "I" can serve God. This spiritualized ego, moved from its obsessions with approval and control, actually begins to merge into the true self. This is another step of the process of self-realization, which results in a more consistent awareness of the Presence of God, and therefore more inner peace.

All these teachings are about becoming free internally in order to leap free externally. You feel compassion for yourself and for others both inside and outside your own being. It's a complete experience that cannot be denied. If you sit in the presence of a true spiritual teacher in any tradition, you actually will feel the atmosphere becoming charged with the presence of God. It's true electricity. The leader may create that environment by leading people into a relationship with God through various forms of prayer. When that feeling of inner and outer freedom becomes more or less permanent within an individual, it is more powerful and more attractive than any type of approval or control that the mind possibly can create or even think about. When the presence of this freedom becomes constant, the feeling is one of previously unthinkable peace and joy.

For most people, however, it is not possible to be constantly in the presence of a spiritual teacher who can create this condition of release and freedom moment after moment. We need tools to keep our minds focused on the sacred, so we use prayer beads, incense and religious statues to keep us inspired. That's why we have the sacred writings. When read in the spirit of devotion, the writings become a vehicle for guidance on experiencing the essence of self and God in union.

Different spiritual traditions practice their own meditations or prayers for releasing. Still, I always keep in mind that no matter how powerfully any such tool seems, it is just a single step on the pathway. This is true of any technique, any meditation. The mind of God is spontaneous and creative, and we ourselves can benefit by holding these qualities in focus at all times. Releasing is one step in a lifetime of steps, and even those who awaken might return to their old ways. We need to be eternally alert in our experience of God. In the words of the ancient Persian poet Haféz, "When people ask, What became of God's light?-simply answer, Awakened beings went back to sleep."

Once again we find ourselves in the heart of all teachings. True devotion to God is necessary to keep us awake and to ensure our ongoing condition of release. Such devotion is our key to continuous awareness, and we must maintain our surrender to God through this devotion at all times.

The need for this level of devotion is expressed beautifully in this poem of Tukaram, the seventeenth century Indian saint:

Take Lord unto thyself
my sense of self and let it vanish utterly.
Take Lord my life.
Live thou my life through me.
I live no longer Lord
but in me now thou livest.
Now between thee and me, my God,
there is no longer room for I and mine.

Meditation

Calling Forth Compassion

Again, as at the end of Chapter Six, we will perform Namasmarana. Begin by chanting the various names of God below, or choose any one name of whichever divine being most resonates with you personally. But this time, prepare for your meditation by holding a picture or perhaps a small statue or some other representative image of your favorite divine being in your hand.

When you pray the name of God while holding in your mind a sacred image that for you contains the energy of God's personality, the expanding power of that prayer begins to spread throughout your being. So if you feel devotion for a particular saint, hold a picture of that being as you pray. Just as you do with a loved one's picture, gaze at the image or press it to your heart. You'll feel something start to move in you. That which is moving is the feeling of compassion, and it will be moving both ways. You will feel the compassion of the saint or deity coming into you, and your own compassion will be flowing out toward that being.

To begin, breathe deeply a few times. As you inhale a deep breath, make sure your abdomen expands outward. When you exhale, the abdomen goes in.

Now chant the name or names of God that open your heart. Here are some names that I love. Use any or all, or choose another from your own tradition.

A-la-ha, Ra-ma, Rah, Ra-pha, Ta-ra.
A-bwoon, Al-lah, A-la-ha, I-nan-na.
Bud-dha, Krish-na, Ish-wa, A-hu-ra.

Remember, the Holy Spirit is the breath of God. Breathe and chant. Grow quiet. Feel the silence. Know that your space within is hallowed out.

Do Namasmarana again, chanting as before. But this time, focus on the picture or small statue of your favorite representation of the Divine that you are holding in your hand. Either close your eyes or open them and gaze as the image. This is a powerful way to create the space for healing energy to flow through you. As you chant, you are developing not just an intellectual relationship, but a relationship that is best described as heart to heart. The heart centers of both you and the being in the picture are being connected. The heart of the Divine is always open and ready.

Place the image in one of both of your hands and hold it over your heart. Breathe and chant a third time. Use whatever names of the Divine appeal to you.

Feel the compassion flowing ever more strongly with each word and each breath.

Again grow silent. Hold the feeling of compassion deep in your consciousness. Feel deeply. Listen deeply. Open yourself to any words coming to you from divine sources. Perhaps you will be informed how to manifest service into your own life.

As always, close with gratitude.

Peace. Amen.

◆   ◆   ◆

10

Ministry of Light

*"The sea of love is not bounded by shores
There is nothing to do but give your life"*

—Haféz

Every human being's work in the world can become a Ministry of Light. Whether we work with a large group of like-minded people or we each stand alone in what may seem a lonesome spiritual environment, the work of the light provides us a singular purpose. As we awaken each morning to the renewal of that purpose, the most inspiring thought I have found is that no matter what task you are called to do, God will perform that task.

Again, this was my personal lesson from India in a nutshell, the ultimate embodiment of wisdom handed down by the great masters through the ages. This primary principle of self-empowerment removes the burdens of the world from our shoulders. When we look to the place that God occupies in our life, we must remember that God is either one hundred percent powerful or not. If we accept that God is totally powerful, then this is obviously the foundation on which to build our everyday lives.

It's just a matter of making the proper connection with God, who is always right in front of our eyes, and that's what we've been talking about throughout this book. Whether we're speaking of the Therapeutae or the Medicine Buddha or the Oneness Movement, the practice of infusing our beings with the light through prayer and meditation and ritual summons the essence of both personal healing and, eventually, world peace. It's truly all about liberation of our beings, liberation from the struggles and pettiness and suffering that come from taking ourselves so seriously that we believe we are personally responsible for changing the world. If each of us can meet the challenge of aligning our own being with the light, that's plenty of accomplishment for one lifetime.

So, start understanding, accepting and utilizing the principle that as you step into the light, you must be ready to embrace the personal liberation of allowing God to do all the work. When you practice the meditations and prayers in this book, or any others of your preference, feel yourself entering into that special feeling of the Divine. As you literally embody Divinity, your thoughts and speech and bodily actions will begin to portray the activity of God. By staying centered in the light, and at the same time centering the light in yourself, you open yourself both to synchronicities forming around you and to your own appropriate and productive reactions to the opportunities offered by those synchronicities. It's all a matter of surrendering to the will of the Divine. Whether for one person and for an entire community, this wonderful and masterful surrender opens the heart into the creation of a Ministry of Light.

During our moments of yielding our need to control in order to surrender to the flow of the universal creative force, we experience life fully. We know that we know that we know that our deepest yearning is to exist in unity with the Divine. If we expand ourselves fearlessly toward our full human capacity, our vision and mentality embraces the essence of the light. This instantly inspires our heartfelt expression of love for God, for ourselves and for all other beings on the planet. Life is at its best and its most exhilarating when we live this way.

Looking around the globe today, we see many spiritual communities of all sizes beginning to bloom. Auroville and the Golden City are among the most widely known of many in India. In the public appearances of his later years in America, Paramahansa Yogananda often called for the creation of "world brotherhood colonies," a system of cooperative communities. This is part of our evolutionary process as humans, part of our future. Oneness is growing. It can't be stopped.

I spoke earlier of the desirability of each person having a spiritual community through which to filter our discernment of God's guidance for our personal pathways. But being among other people serves many other purposes as well. It keeps us from getting lost in our own thoughts and from feeling separated or alone in the world. It allows us to interact with our fellow beings in joy and happiness, and to seek solace during times of sadness and grief. Community enables us to keep the full spectrum of life in our vision so that we do not inadvertently sink into our individual fantasies about how we and other humans should or should not be acting. It liberates our minds from the inner poisons of expectation, comparison and judgment.

Creating a Ministry of Light actually can be anyone's purpose. Your purpose, if you are wondering what to do during this lifetime, just do this. Do it this moment. It doesn't matter if you're alone, or a member of a church, or among a few friends who will join you. Create your ministry by simply declaring you feel the call to do so. You don't have to call it a ministry; call it a life focus or a mission or whatever. Next, let go of any feeling of responsibility to achieve any particular goals. This is the same as hallowing out the space for God to come in and act. Then, as Solomon did when he prayed for the people at the dedication of the temple, call in the light. This is a meditative procedure that you can accomplish in this very instant. As you do this, prepare to be amazed at what will come to you.

In order to allow your ministry to develop, simply hold true to your vision and be ready for anything. If it feels right to speak to others about your work, do so. If not, keep your own counsel. But do stay in touch with the light. Hold God in your heart, and remember the one and only doctrine: love God, love others, love yourself. As you watch your life change, you well may see a mission attaching itself to your declaration of your Ministry of light. In time, a clear vision of your pathway will emerge. Throughout all this process, your are developing your own inner pathway to personal healing and global peace. At any time you want to practice discernment in terms of whether you are still on track, here is an outline of seven spiritual principles that always will be present, obvious and at work in any Ministry of light, no matter if that ministry is in its infancy or maturity, or if it consists of one person or many. This list can be referred to at any time, whenever you want to evaluate your group's or your own alignment with the sacred light of healing.

Seven Principles of a Ministry of Light

1. Caring for the heart.

This is an amazing time to be alive. Airplanes carry us halfway around the world in only a few hours. We write e-mails to those same destinations and they're delivered instantaneously. Doctors hold at their fingertips an astounding array of technology and research to influence our physical health, before, during and after our illnesses. Televised news informs us immediately of our planet's crucial events such as natural disasters and wars. Once in a while, there's some good news too, such as how we help one another during desperate moments. We are efficient, informed and in touch. Most of us eat very well. This is all marvelous, and I for one like my comfort and harbor no desire to return a more primitive lifestyle. But still, there is no denying that all the material richness in the world is not enough to provide a life of true fulfillment for any person. No matter how much we as a culture advance and prosper in the material realm, one essential question eternally confronts us:

What of the heart?

Coming to know the light as real, not in symbolic or metaphoric terms, we understand that sacred perception and use of the light for healing is the answer to this question of the heart.

To put it simply, the light will take care of the heart. As soon as we humans realize and practice this fully, we will find ourselves living in an even more marvelous time. We will no longer obsess fanatically on what we must do, how perfectly we must do it, and how quickly we must finish so that we can do something else just as perfectly and quickly, and on and on and on. Instead, we will learn to hold a constant focus on the light, feeling the heart fully open. Then we simply will allow life to come to us and flow through us as an unimpeded succession of synchronous events. This is how we are meant to live.

This easy grace brings exhilaration, and this is how God intends us to live. As we become proficient in this grace, the heart begins to function fully as an open organ of wisdom, compassion and love.

2. Light is love, and love is light. It's one thing, not two.

In essence, God gives us a role to play in a dynamic drama called life and invites us to improvise as we see fit. The nature of our improvisation determines the quality of the life we live. If we improvise love, we live a life of love. Why would we want to live any other way? But in order to create this new and more powerful future, both personal and universal, we must release whatever is holding us immobile in the present. Releasing means we must surrender to God's plan for us. That means letting go of what or who we think we are supposed to be. Surrender has been the story of mystics since time began, the yielding to the Divine and then the soaring beyond limits.

While watching Celebrating Life grow around me over the years, I have experienced both up times and down times. There were many moments along the way when I prayed and meditated deeply in search of a more profound understanding of what was happening. I was moved to continue my walk by words like these from Padre Pio, the Italian stigmatist who has served as my Spirit guide for many years: "Don't waste energy on things that generate worry, anxiety and anguish. Only one thing is necessary: Lift up your spirit and love God."

In other words, release, surrender, hallow out a space, receive the Holy Spirit and do your work. No matter how complex I tried to make my life, it always returned to this basic simplicity.

For me, the emergence and existence of Celebrating Life demonstrates the power and potential of this mystical pathway. But this should not surprise us. Explaining and demonstrating this pathway of light is the work of all spiritual teachers. As we realize the light, we feel love. They go together. It's that simple.

This is one aspect of what I mean when I say that the mission of Jesus still has not been accomplished. It's ongoing. As people come to realize that Holy Spirit is alive and well in the world and is capable of working for us on every level, one more step in Jesus' mission is taken. But still, that mission will project into the future. That's why we continue to pray and live with simplicity and devotion. That is how we send the light forward to future generations. That's how we love perpetually. That's how we rise above our perceived human limitations. In the words of Saint Francis of Assisi, "Above all the grace and the gifts that Christ gives to his beloved is that of overcoming self." As this small self or ego is overcome, then our true inner nature, our inherent Divinity, arises to fill the space that our personal devotional practice has hallowed out.

3. Faith is the energy to command.

Haleh Pourafzal was a Persian mystic and a monk in our Spirit of Peace Monastic Community before she crossed over into the Spirit Realm in 2002. Haleh grew up in Iran, immersed in the ancient teachings of her homeland. Her spirit guide was the Persian poet Haféz, and she displayed the depths of her own discernment in articulating the mastery of the poet in her book, *Haféz: Teachings of the Philosopher of Love.* Haleh also was a gifted poet and writer herself. In her writings, we find this observation:

> The being of a mystic should be deeply empty and sufficiently expanded in order to see, feel and be One with the entirety of the infinite universe and with the Creator. In this state of being, a mystic can be God's worker as teacher, healer, oracle and manifestor of the Divine Beauty from wave reality into particle reality.

As Haleh speaks in quantum theory terms of moving from wave reality to particle reality, she is describing the process of bringing the highest spiritual qualities of joy, peace and unconditional love from the realm of theory into the realm of our daily life. This is the mystical way of articulating the basic truth now being confirmed daily by science, that we humans can make changes in our physical world through our meditations and prayers and thoughts. We are capable of commanding our own health. We also can command peace for our planet.

This ability of the human mind to effect changes in its physical environment lies at the heart of both ancient mystical experience and modern quantum theory. Gary Zukov addresses this relationship in *The Dancing Wu-Li Masters*. He writes:

> A powerful awareness lies dormant in these discoveries: a discovery of the hitherto-unsuspected powers of the mind to mold 'reality,' rather than the other way around. In this sense, the philosophy of physics is becoming indistinguishable from the philosophy of Buddhism, which is the philosophy of enlightenment.

Confirmation of this parallel mystical relationship comes in these words of the Dalai Lama: "Both science and the teachings of the Buddha relate to us the fundamental unity of all beings." When the Dalai Lama left Tibet for India in 1959, it is reported that his last prayer in his native land was the ancient chant known as the Heart *Sutra* (teaching), composed by Indian monks around the time of Jesus. This teaching is said to convey the essence an oral tradition called the *Prajna Paramita*, or the Perfection of Wisdom, which dates back to the era of the historical Buddha. Here is a central passage of this sutra:

Form is no different from emptiness.
Emptiness is no different from form.
Form is precisely emptiness.
Emptiness is precisely form.

These simple lines of wisdom have provided fodder for meditation for many centuries of Buddhists. The apparent contradictions in the concepts serve as a gateway for realization that the world as we see it is not necessarily the totality of existence. The contradictions force us to shift into our nonintellectual perception. As we travel beyond the mind's third dimensional perceptions, we see that this dissolution of the distinction between form and emptiness is simply the dissolution of duality. In other words, let us stop obsessing over the need to see everything as right or wrong, as positive or negative. The ultimate message of the sutra is that deeper perception about God and life is available to us as something more profound than that which presents itself in our everyday reality. If our full focus centers on love of God and service to our fellow beings, the truth is we will have no time to waste on making futile judgments about other humans, their beliefs and their activities. As our focus shifts away from the need to judge others, it shifts toward the realization of the ever-present opportunity to go forth fully empowered with the faith to command positive changes in our existence.

4. It's not about doctrine.

The Persian poet Haféz points directly to abandoning the intellectual approach to God when he writes: "Throw away your books to study in this school, for no book explains the science of love."

All traditions practice their own rituals and sacred ceremonies as energetic tools to experience God. These practices are gifts to us from the spirit world, and each gift takes a slightly different form. Still, there is a single purpose for the rituals and the sacred ceremonies of the Native Americans in their various languages, the Roman Catholics, the Hindus in Sanskrit and the Orthodox Churches that still speak the Aramaic. This single purpose is the personal experience of God. These ceremonies are performed so that we can experience the tangible presence of the Divine. If we walk away from these events and, for whatever reason, we have not experienced God, that's a big waste of effort. You may as well be watching television because you are wasting valuable time. My work has never been about condemning any tradition or declaring one way is wrong and another way is right. My mission is simply to say, "Look, let's get back to the essence of all of these traditions, the experience of the Divine." These practices become beneficial when understood in that way.

It is easy for people get hung up on form as the most important ingredient of rituals and ceremonies. If a ritual is performed but the energy is not released for an experience, people get dismayed. They start looking for other religions. They start doubting that God exists. But what didn't happen was the release of the sacred energy, and that's the whole purpose of the ritual. It's easy to blame the form, to say it wasn't done right. But there are many different forms and people experience healing many different ways, so there has to be something else that makes the difference. Some people will say it's the intention that matters most. Some say it's the faith. But the ultimate, simple truth is there has to be a connection with the Divine, and that connection is accomplished through devotion.

Consider Mother Theresa's quote, "I believe in person to person. Every person is Christ for me, and since there is only one Jesus, that person is the one person in the world at that moment." In other words, Mother Theresa saw a purity in every person, in every single being that she helped during her many years of service. She refused to get hung up on form. Otherwise, how could she have gone on with such remarkable work? For her, the one pure thing she saw was Jesus. This was her authentic vision that enabled her to perform her mission in the world. Your own one pure thing may be some other aspect of Divinity, your own personal inspiration from a saint or deity. Each of us can receive such a vision, if only we are willing to surrender to God and learn to see through and beyond that which everyday reality considers to be solid form.

5. Prayer can change the physical reality of life.

Authentic prayer does not involve begging or pleading desperately with God. Rather, it is speaking and listening to the Divine in the sacred stillness of hallowed silence. Or as is often more preferable, simply listening, willingly receiving. Prayer articulates gratitude and inspires us to open to guidance from Holy Spirit and the Holy Spirits. It acknowledges the power of light and initiates the feeling of Divinity within our beings. True prayer initiates a relationship with universal awareness that comes to us as the Presence. That Presence brings healing and peace in unlimited application to all of life.

One of the greatest laments I continually hear year after year from very sincere people, even "churchgoing" people, is, "I don't know how to pray." Many people were never taught how simple this spiritual conversation can be. One of the best and simplest set of directions for prayer comes from the New Testament in Phillipians 4:

> Do not be anxious about anything, but in everything, by prayer and petition, with thanksgiving, present your requests to God. And the peace of God, which transcends all understanding, will guard your hearts and your minds in Christ Jesus.

After making your request or intention known, release it. Let it go with words of gratitude and thanks. Let it go and let it flow into the universe. Feel the release, feel the power and joy of connecting with God. Feel the resonance of your own prayer as it travels to God. Researchers now are saying that the human heart creates the signals that in turn tell our brain what vibrations to send to our physical beings. The quality of the signal from the heart, these theories say, either affirms or denies life in our bodies. Further, the mechanism that regulates the quality of the signal appears to be how we feel about life in any given moment. If I feel at peace, my heart sends that essence to the brain and it then travels onward to the physical being.

In simple terms, prayer is a state of being rather than action. There is a passage in the Gospel of Mark that is translated differently in the St. Joseph Bible than in any other translation. In all other versions I've read, it goes: "And Jesus went out into the wilderness, and he prayed." But in the St. Joseph version, that passage reads: "And Jesus went out into the wilderness where he was absorbed in prayer."

That difference in wording creates a tremendous difference in meaning, and I believe the St. Joseph version captures the true meaning. To be absorbed in prayer indicates a state of being, not doing. This involves precisely what we have been discussing: releasing, surrendering, hallowing out a space, welcoming the Holy Spirit into that space and realizing the presence of your true, authentic self. It is in this condition of being that physical healing takes place beyond the defined boundaries of medical science. It is also in this condition that each of us as an individuated consciousness experiences the feeling that we call peace.

When enough people attain this state of being through prayer and meditation and hold that feeling with such conviction that it begins to spread out into the world, even our political leaders will start to pick up the nature and intent of that feeling. Leaders who establish policies that shape the future and direction of our nations and the world will come to perceive and respond to this peaceful intent. Of course, many leaders already are proclaiming that they want to choose and champion the ways of peace, but their actions do not reflect their words. Once they begin to feel what the people feel, however, the leaders' actions quite naturally will evolve into policies designed to maintain that essence of peace.

This is such a powerful pathway of influencing leaders into positive action that it actually does not even require that the leaders participate directly in creating or understanding this state of being. If they can feel the people's intent in their hearts, they will respond. One way of describing the workings of this process is to think of throwing a pebble into a pond, as in our earlier meditation, and then watching the ripples spread out in all directions. Who can say where or when the ripples will stop? Do they simply stop when our eyes no longer see them forming and moving? No. The ripple effect would travel much, much further than the eye can follow. No one can know how far. Each one of our thoughts, words and deeds is like that. So if we embody our thoughts and words in the sacred power of prayer, the pebbles of our peaceful intent are cast with great force into the pond to create ripples that spread and spread and spread.

I have written extensively in previous books on the various kinds of prayer, and I suggest reading *Prayer and the Five Stages of Healing* and *The Healing Path of Prayer* if you want to study in more depth.

6. True enlightenment is an ongoing state of being, not a momentary experience.

When we speak of enlightenment, there are two different conditions we may be referring to. One is a momentary happening, a brief flashing of higher awareness. The other is a permanent change, a full shift of our wiring for God. In the condition of full and lasting enlightenment, each person literally becomes a different being. That new being's awareness is focused fully on God, and both the pleasures and struggles of the everyday world fade into mere happenings. We cease to perceive daily events as blessings or curses, good or evil. We suddenly no longer care who we are, but at the same time we know what we are to do. The pathway to Divinity appears clear and steady, right in front of us. But to achieve this condition, we may have to travel through times of forceful inner challenges.

I often speak and write about the Dark Night of the Soul, a phrase created by Saint John of the Cross, the sixteenth century

Spanish monk and mystic philosopher. John, who knew whereof he spoke because he was writing while imprisoned for following his inner knowingness in terms of his own faith, was referring to those periods of our lives that seem so embedded with darkness that we become engulfed in hopelessness and the feeling that God has abandoned us. Our lives are in crisis. Depression sets in. We cannot see the light. We may be going through a serious illness or attending to a loved one who is. There seems to be no answer. But it is at these very times of trial that, if we rely on our faith and wisdom, we have the opportunity to let go of our struggles and to connect in a vibrant new way to God's will and plan. A new experience of personal reality replaces the old. Truly, it's like being reborn. We find within our beings a previously unknown fluidity. We enter a process of inner development consistent with the teachings of the mystics and with contemporary science as well. At some point, we start feeling better. As we emerge from the darkness, we find great light awaiting us. Again, we can draw courage and inspiration from the sacred writings. The Persian poet Haféz writes of his own pathway: "Haféz, weakened by poverty, alone in the dark, this night is your pathway into the light. Don't despair, walk on."

Today, we are challenged to see the whole world as passing through its own Dark Night. The entire human family is being challenged, now as never before, to manifest its way out of the violence and tragedy that is being projected onto us by the conditions of our contemporary world. No matter how bombarded we are by newscasts of disasters and the resulting fears of our friends and family, we must know that this is the very moment of realizing in our innermost beings that the light is still out there.

This arousal from the darkness is reflected in the well-known command of the Indian mystic Sri Aurobindo: "Arise, transcend thyself. Thou art human and the whole nature of humanity is to become more than oneself." In other words, don't settle for that which is presented to you by the outer world as being the way we must live. It truly is in our nature to see and be something more, to see the possibility of divine healing and peace and to be that possibility manifesting into actual reality. This transcendence is the nature of a permanent state of enlightenment.

7. Authentic peace is not the absence of war, but rather the presence of Divinity.

Just as authentic health is not simply the absence of disease, but rather the presence of vibrant well being, authentic peace is not just the absence of armed conflict. In the space where conflict has subsided, the Divine must become real.

We must realize that living in the light means a new way of life. To establish sustainability in spiritual pursuit, we cannot return to our old ways of being. Physical, emotional and spiritual healing are not an end in themselves, but rather they are a means to a sacred end. We heal ourselves so that we can heal the planet.

"I was once asked why I don't participate in antiwar demonstrations," Mother Theresa commented during an interview late in her life. "I said that I will never do that, but as soon as you have a pro-peace rally, I'll be there."

Mother Theresa's point is that there is a huge difference between a reactive stance and the positive projection of a sacred image. Nonviolence, if not authentic, doesn't work. Unless a person is totally committed in his or her deepest being, that person is not prepared to maintain the necessary composure as trials become more and more difficult in the practice of nonviolence. If nonviolence exists merely as a doctrine within a person's mind, it will be very difficult for that person to sustain through the demands of this pathway. It is relatively easy to sit peacefully until confronted and perhaps abused by an authority figure. There's no challenge in just sitting. But if the true feeling and clarity of purpose is not running through every nerve and fiber of one's being, that person sooner or later will react to the opposition is such a way as to increase rather than decrease the violence of the situation. To be effective, nonviolence must become an authentic spiritual force in which the individual is totally infused, and it is difficult for people to reach this level of authenticity through a brief period of training, as is usually offered before demonstrations.

When nonviolence is authentic, as it was in Gandhi, it can change the world. The same can be said of simply praying for peace. It is up to each individual to prepare through personal growth and awakening for the challenge of entering the process of generating peace in just the right way and at just the right time throughout our planet. This is the meaning of the clever spiritual advice: "Choose one or the other: (1) don't just sit there, do something, or (2) don't just do something, sit there."

Each of us can activate or meditate. It is our choice. But the point is always to bring peace, not just oppose war. If we trust God to perform that which we are called to do, why not extend that trust to creating peace on our planet? And we do that through the many ways we have explored in this book. Prayer. Silence. Meditation. Communion with the Divine. Chanting the names of God. The pure practice of the light is true nonviolence, and the resulting peace can manifest in endless ways in our lives. One of the simplest yet most profound poem prayers calling forth this peace comes from Saint Claire of Assisi:

> Place your mind before the mirror of eternity,
> place your soul in the brightness of His glory,
> place your heart in the image of the divine essence
> and transform yourself by contemplation
> utterly into the image of his divinity
> that you too may feel what his friends feel as they taste
> the hidden sweetness that God himself has set aside
> from the beginning for those who love him.

From this singular focus on the Divine, peace ripples outward into its universal potential. This is the path of prayer into peace.

Meditation

A Prayer for Oneness

Here is my own prayer for the Oneness Movement in America. May its power ripple out through all the world. May it touch every being. May it bring the Sacred light of Healing to you personally. As always, breathe deeply. Relax. You may wish to reread Saint Claire's poem, above, to help create a sacred mood. Then say this prayer with me. Repeat it three times. Then three more. And then as often and as many times as you know that you know that you know is appropriate.

Come, Holy Spirit
Living flame of love
Kindle in us the fire of your Divine Presence
That all may be One in joy

Thank you for meditating and praying with me throughout this journey. Thank you for being open to sharing my perceptions, and for infusing into yourself and all others the essence of the Holy Spirit for our healing and for the world's enlightenment. It is time for us all to go forth, manifesting well being and creating peace through the Divine Light. This is a wondrous time of incredible opportunity. Let us travel together into our sacred work, knowing that God's blessings flow through us at all times.

Let us travel together into Oneness.

Ron Roth

◆   ◆   ◆

Appendix

❖

(As referenced in Chapter 2)

The Neurobiology of Awakening to Oneness
by Christian Opitz

One of my favorite questions to ask an audience is, "How many times in your life have you been wrong?" Of course, nobody ever can give a reasonable answer to this question. Experience shows that our sense of reality is pretty unreliable. Yet whenever we are convinced about something, a new strongly held opinion, we again project a sense of reality onto it as if we had never erred before.

The human brain has a simple mechanism it follows in trying to determine what reality is. The more neurological intensity there is, the more the feeling, thought or experience correlating with that particular neurological pattern will feel real to us. People who suffer from OCD (obsessive compulsive disorder) often know rationally that their obsessive behavior makes no sense, but a part of their primitive survival brain, the basal ganglia, produces such strong neurological firing that they feel the need to engage in these patterns. The same principle is at work, perhaps in a less dramatic fashion, in the experience of life for all people. If a biological urge in the brain with intense neurological firing is at odds with a mental insight, the biological urge will be the stronger factor in determining a person's sense of reality.

This mechanism of projecting a subjective sense of reality according to neurological intensity opens the door to a deep understanding of spiritual awakening. All spiritual traditions are attempting to free human beings from suffering. From a neurological perspective, suffering feels so real to us, simply because certain parts of the brain that are designed for struggle and not for joy, are chronically overactive. Boredom, fear, emotional pain, inner conflict, feelings of inadequacy, loneliness, feeling separate from other people, life, God, all these states of consciousness coincide with intense neurological activity in certain parts of the brain and lack of activity in others.

The Overactivity of Neurological Survival Patterns

According to Dr. Paul MacLean, former director of the Laboratory of Brain Evolution and Behavior, we actually have three brains in one. The three levels of brain development that Dr. MacLean describes are the reptilian brain, the mammalian brain or limbic system and the neocortex, our higher brain, which includes the very important frontal lobes.

The Reptilian Brain and Parietal Lobes

The reptilian brain is responsible for simple survival functions. When there is an actual threat to our physical survival, the reptilian brain creates the well-documented fight or flight response. This part of the brain derives its name from the fact that this level of brain development is found in all reptiles. The problem for us human beings is that our reptilian brain is chronically overactive and therefore governs aspects of our lives it is not at all useful for. Reptilian life is simple. It is concerned with survival and probably not much else. Reptiles don't have fun, they don't engage in any behavior that could qualify as playing. They do not engage in emotional bonding. Mating is strictly for procreation, offspring are not raised. Eggs are laid and then the kids have to look out for themselves. All this is perfect if you are a lizard, but for human beings with slightly more complex lives, the reptilian brain is a poor instrument. Yet its chronic overactivity expands the authority of the reptilian brain and we are governed by its survival patterns in our relationships, in our experience of life itself and even in our spiritual search.

The parietal lobes, located at the back of the head are a functional extension of the reptilian brain. Although anatomically different, the parietal lobes work together with the reptilian brain to create a very basic, primitive sense of self. One function of the parietal lobes is to give us a sense of our physical boundaries. This is very important if we want to be able to walk, pick up something with our hand or put clothes on, we need to know the difference between our body and its environment. But as an extension of the overactive reptilian brain, the parietal lobes are equally chronically overactive in people. With a high level of neurological intensity in the part of the brain that gives us a sense of physical separation, the feeling of separation is experienced as very real. It is then projected not only onto the body, but onto the sense of existing itself. Overactive parietal lobes are the neurological foundation for the separate ego, the limited identification of oneself with the body, one's personal life story and experiences as if they belong to a permanent central character. As Dr. D'Aquili and Dr. Newberg, authors of the highly acclaimed book *Why God won't go away* have shown, experiences of oneness are mediated by a decrease in parietal lobe activity.

The Frontal Lobes

The frontal lobes are the physical anchor for transcendence. If activated in a coherent way, the frontal lobes allow for the experience of oneness with all things and with God, causeless love and compassion, unshakable inner peace and freedom. In almost all people, the frontal lobes are either chronically underactive or sporadically activated in a discoherent way. Stimulating drugs such as cocaine or certain neurological disorders such as stuttering and hallucinations can activate the frontal lobes, but these neurological processes are uncoordinated and obviously do not lead to spiritual awakening. A harmonious awakening of the frontal lobes has to be based on a reduction of reptilian brain/parietal lobe activity; otherwise, the ongoing overactivity in the brain's survival centers will allow only a chaotic and short-lived frontal lobe surge. Underactive frontal lobes lead to a life experience that is deadening, boring, desperate. Henry David Thoreau was probably talking about the effects of underactive frontal lobes when he wrote, "Most people live lives of silent despair and desperate mediocrity." It just doesn't feel right and therefore we have invented whole industries for delivering short-term stimulation.

The need for a deactivation of the parietal lobes as a foundation for frontal lobe activation has another important component. In the human experience, there is an inherent yearning for something more, beyond the limitations of the relative world. Often that yearning is projected onto the mind in the hope to become a master of one's life, being able to create an experience of infinity, abundance. Much of the idea about positive thinking reflects this projection of our deepest inner yearning onto the illusion that the mind of a person is infinitely powerful. If you have a chance to spend time with paranoid people who quickly see that thoughts don't create reality. People suffering from paranoia are obsessed with thinking about calamities that never happen to them. Hypochondriac people have better health statistics than the average population, yet they tend to believe that every little ache they feel is cancer. In a world of untold dimensions and forces, our own mental constructs are a rather small factor. Also, the manifested world has inherent limitations. If the eight finalists of the Olympic 100-meter dash all mentally "create" victory, there is still only going to be one gold medalist in the end. But the yearning for a transcendent, limitless reality is present within us. When the frontal lobes get activated to some degree, it can feel very empowering. If such an experience is not based in a deactivation of the parietal lobes, this feeling of empowerment will be most likely interpreted as a personal trait, as if there is a central character that is now all-powerful. Many spiritual teachers describe and warn about the spiritual ego. If our parietal lobes are not deactivated first, inspiration, experiences of high energy and higher consciousness will in some way feed the sense of a separate self, only now we have a separate self on steroids. For balanced spiritual awakening, the illusion of separation has to be dissolved. The vast, empty space of consciousness that results can then be filled with the Divine Presence, which is anchored in a person's experience through activating the frontal lobes.

Putting Diksha to the Test

When I first heard about Sri Bhagavan's teachings and his statement that diksha deactivates the parietal lobes and activates the frontal lobes, it sounded almost too good to be true. So I wanted to see if these changes could be detected in a reproducible way in people receiving diksha. To make sure that the results of my research were not due to some anomaly, I joined forces with Ralf Franziskowski, M.D., an experienced doctor in the field of psychosomatic medicine. We went to Golden City, the center of the Oneness Movement and performed tests on many people in different stages of the process of awakening induced by diksha. We used two very different devices, an electromagnetic sensor that scans a person's energy field and another device measuring electrical resistance in the skin, which is then correlated with different physiological functions.

The results where simply miraculous. Everybody who had been receiving diksha for about one year showed a decrease in parietal lobe activity that has previously been detected only in a few highly advanced meditators with over ten thousand hours of meditation experience and in a few Zen masters and shamans. The people we tested had been doing their share of spiritual seeking before, but they were ordinary people. The stress parameters in all of them where exceptionally low. We continued to test these people as they where going through an intensive course in Golden City, and the neuro-biological restructuring kept going on with amazing efficiency. Stress patterns were reduced even more to a remarkable degree. Frontal lobe activity increased significantly and always with a slight dominance of the left frontal lobe. This is the signature pattern for healthy frontal lobe activation. If there is right frontal lobe dominance, delusions and depression can be the result, so I was glad to see that everybody receiving deeksha showed a dominance of left frontal lobe activity.

These results are reproducible. Everybody we have tested so far shows a tremendous neuro-biological restructuring and harmonization through diksha. It is remarkable that this process works for people no matter what their background is. Personality traits, spiritual beliefs and lifestyle all seem irrelevant. The grace of diksha apparently is infinitely generous and capable to liberate people from the confines of neurological survival stress and the illusion of a separate self.

In more advanced stages of this process, there is a profound awakening of a communication loop between the frontal lobe and the heart. It has been known for a while that the human heart muscle contains tens of thousands of neurons, a little brain franchise right in the heart. These neurons become much more active when people awaken to the experience of universal love and compassion. When I was asked to examine Ron Roth, this brain-heart connection stood out as most impressive. I found similar results in Sri Ananda Giri and Sri Samadarshini, two of the senior teachers at the Oneness University who live in exceptionally advanced states of consciousness. I truly believe that in people like Ron, Sri Anandagiri and Sri Samadarshini, the potential of the future of humanity has become reality. The elevated brain-heart connection in these remarkable teachers shows that it is possible for humanity to awaken to an experience of universal love beyond our wildest dreams.

How does it work?

I do not believe that science can truly understand divine grace. There is however, a neuro-biological explanation that can help us to understand why divine grace can be transmitted through such a simple process and have such profound effects on the brain. When you see someone perform a task, say reaching out for a cup and grabbing it, you know instantly what that person is doing. This understanding does not require any conscious thought. You know what the other person is doing because of the activity of mirror cells in the brain. When the other person is reaching for the cup, certain neurons in your brain get activated that mirror the neurological activity the other person produces in order to move the arm. You know what they are doing, because your own brain simulates their neurological firing sequence.

Now imagine someone in your presence is in a state of consciousness where divine grace is consciously present in them in a very deep way. The activity in their brain that is caused by the divine energies will be mirrored in your brain. Your brain will "get" what a state of grace is like, due to this mirroring effect. This phenomenon of neurological resonance is probably one of the mechanisms behind the effectiveness of diksha.

Resonance or entrainment was first discovered by Christian Huygens in 1668, when he found that two mechanical clocks, if placed in a certain proximity, will align their rhythms until they match completely. What is rarely mentioned about the phenomenon of entrainment is that a harmonious rhythm is always the stronger, prevailing one when two rhythms come together. Harmony and balance entrains disharmony to its own level. When someone is initiated to give diksha, their brain has access to this most benevolent, gracious energy. In giving diksha, this energy manifests through the neurons of the diksha giver, which turn into a tuning fork, entraining the brain of the receiving person to the same experience of grace.

There is certainly a lot more that is happening through diksha and most of it is beyond my understanding. The more facets of this phenomenon I discover, the more it shows me what an infinite mystery it is. Science will never fully understand the workings of the Divine, but perhaps some of these concepts can help us to deepen our understanding.

The Potential for Global Awakening

Sri Bhagavan has repeatedly pointed out that a decrease in the earth's magnetic field is one of the reasons why it is now possible for humanity at large to undergo a global awakening to oneness. There are several aspects to the magnetic field of the earth, the one that is of interest here is the dipolar moment. Simply put, this is the degree of polarity between the north and south poles, or the degree of dualistic tension in the earth. Over the last two hundred years there has been a significant decrease in the dipolar moment. This is evidenced by coherence of magnetic particle in volcanic lava. When hot lava cools down and solidifies, the magnetic particles in it entrain to the earth's magnetic field. The degree of coherence in these particles in a piece of lava indicates the strength of the dipolar moment. The stronger it is, the more coherent these particles will be. In lava that comes out of the earth today, this coherence is far less pronounced than in lava that came out of the earth two hundred years ago. The same observation can be made with magnetic particles in pottery of today compared to pottery made two hundred years ago.

Our brain has its share of magnetic particles, especially magnetite, a form of iron oxide found in the pineal gland, the frontal lobes and the ethmoid bones. Through magnetite in our brain, the earth's magnetic field exercises a stabilizing effect on the way our brain organizes experiences. This process is in itself completely neutral. But if humanity is in a global state of survival struggle and separation consciousness, this will also be stabilized through the dipolar moment. The decrease of the dipolar moment is now opening the gates of global consciousness for the awakening to oneness. It can certainly cause some disorientation as a healthy healing crisis of consciousness, but this destabilization of the old structures of separation is necessary for oneness to become our conscious reality.

A decrease of the dipolar moment to a zero point and a resulting pole shift is not new for humanity. The last polar shift occurred around 800 BCE. In ancient China, compass technology has been around since 1000 B.C. At that time, these compasses pointed north. But in 800 BCE their needles shifted and since then are pointing south. This is remarkable evidence for a complete shift of polarity in the earth.

After 800 BCE, humanity took a very different turn. In Homer's epic *Odysseus*, probably authored shortly after 800 BCE, the hero fights for his independence from the gods. In all Greek epics and tales from before, humans were only string puppets of the gods. Within a few centuries, Greek culture began to develop science, democracy as a political principle and a rich variety of arts and culture. The philosophical outlook changed from a naïve, childlike belief in anthropomorphic gods to a variety of worldviews, based on human reason. The Greek culture is just one of many examples of how the last polar shift was the beginning of an individuation process of the human psyche. Tribal consciousness gave way to an increased individual consciousness. This mirrors the development of a human being, growing into a sense of an individual self in the natural course of growing up. This is a natural process. According to Sri Bhagavan, in young adulthood, this individual self would once again dissolve into oneness, if the human brain would function naturally.

I believe as a species, we human beings have done enough now to experience our separate sense of self. A new pole shift is approaching and it seems logical that it marks humanity's reawakening to oneness. In all my searching, the power of the diksha is the most powerful catalyst for this awakening I have found. It is certainly not coincidence that a divine incarnation like Sri Amma and Sri Bhagavan is occurring at the time of this polar shift. From everything I have seen, I come to the conclusion that the liberating power of diksha will play a vital role in our collective awakening to become one human family of love and oneness again.

Bibliography

Campbell, Joseph, *The Inner Reaches of Outer Space: Metaphor as Myth and as Religion.* (Harper Perennial).

Campbell, Joseph, in Conversation with Michael Toms, *An Open Life* (Larson).

Emoto, Masaru, *The Hidden Messages in Water* (Beyond Words).

Easwaran, Eknath (Editor), *The Bhagavad Gita,* (Nilgiri Press).

Easwaran, Eknath (Translator), The Upanishads (Nilgiri Press).

Francis, T. Dayanandan, *The Mission and Message of Ramalinga Swamy* (Motilal Banarsass of Delhi).

Gandhi, Mahatma, *The Essential Gandhi: An Anthology of His Writings on His Life, Work, and Ideas* (Vintage).

Heart Sutra; The Prajna Paramita (Friedman/Fairfax).

Hildegard of Bingen, *Scivias* (Paulist Press).

His Holiness The Dalai Lama, *Dzogchen: The Heart Essence of the Great Perfection* (Snow Lion).

Judeus, Philo, *The Contemplative Life. (Various translations)*

Lama Zopa Rinpoche, *Ultimate Healing: The Power of Compassion* (Wisdom).

Lao-Tsu, *Tao Te Ching* (Sacred Books of the East).

Mother Theresa, *Simple Path* (Ballantine).

Mary, Francis, *Padre Pio: The Wonder Worker* (Ignatius Press).

Paramahansa Yogananda, *Autobiography of a Yogi* (Self-Realization Fellowship).

Paramahansa Yogananda, *Songs of the Soul* (Self-Realization Fellowship).

Pourafzal, Haleh, and Roger Montgomery, *Haféz: Teachings of the Philosopher of Love* (Inner Traditions International).

Ranade, Ramchandra, *Tukaram* (SUNY Press).

Rigopoulas, Antonio, *The Life and Teachings of Sai Baba of Shirdi* (SUNY Series in Religious Studies).

Roth, Ron, with Peter Occhiogrosso, *Holy Spirit for Healing: Merging Ancient Wisdom with Modern Medicine* (Hay House).

Roth, Ron, with Peter Occhiogrosso, *Prayer and the Five Stages of Healing* (Hay House.

Roth, Ron, with Peter Occhiogrosso, *The Healing Path of Prayer; A Modern Mystic's Guide to Spiritual Power* (Hay House).

Saint Francis of Assisi, *The Writings of St. Francis of Assisi* (Franciscan Press).

Sathya Sai Baba, *Namasmarana: A Universal Sadhana,* (Sri Sathya Sai Books).

Savoy, Gene, *The Essaei Document: Secrets of an Eternal Race* (The International Community of Christ.

Sri Aurobindo, *The Life Divine* (Lotus Press).

Sri Bhagavan, *Evenings ... with Sri Bhagavan* (Oneness University).

Vermes, Geza and Martin D. Goodman, editors, *The Essenes according to the Classical Sources.* (Sheffield: Oxford Centre for Postgraduate Hebrew Studies and JSOT Press).

About the Authors

Modern-day mystic Ron Roth has brought healing to thousands through a powerful spiritual grace that came to him more than thirty years ago. People of many faiths and traditions have traveled great distances from throughout the world to attend his events in the United States. But as Ron always reminds everyone, "God heals. I do not." Ron served as a Roman Catholic Priest for twenty-five years before founding Celebrating Life Ministries, and he holds a Ph.D. in Religious Studies.

Ron is author of *The Healing Path of Prayer; Prayer and The Five Stages of Healing; Holy Spirit: Boundless Energy of God; I Want to See Jesus in a New Light: Healing Reflections for People of All Faiths; Holy Spirit for Healing: Merging Ancient wisdom with Modern Medicine; and Reclaim Your Spiritual Power.* He has recorded many audio and videotapes, CDs and DVDs.

Roger Montgomery is co-author of *Haféz: Teachings of the Philosopher of Love* and author of *Twenty Count: Sacred Mathematics of Awakening.* He is a teacher of awareness disciplines associated with the Buddha and a frequent speaker at global peace gatherings.

Order and Contact Information

You can order Ron Roth's other books, Cd's and DVD's from
Isaac Bookstore:
Website: www.ronroth.com
Email: paulclr@theramp.net

To receive a free audio download of the Sun Meditation go to:
www.thepowerofqs.com

To contact Roger Montgomery:

The Power of Q's.com
2233 W Baseline Rd Ste C-103
Tempe, AZ 85284

Phone: 602-956-7171

Email: info@thepowerofqs.com
Website: www.powerofqs.com

978-0-595-69059-
0-595-69059-9

CPSIA information can be obtained
at www.ICGtesting.com
Printed in the USA
LVHW030406210520
656014LV00004B/40/J

9 780595 690596